PEOPLE OF MY JOURNEY

By the Reverend Arthur H. Holt

South Carolina United Methodist Advocate Press

Copyright © 2023 by South Carolina United Methodist Advocate Press

All rights reserved. No part of this book may be reproduced or transmitted in any form or by any means, electronic or mechanical, including photocopying, recording or by any information storage and retrieval system, without permission in writing from the Publisher.

First published in the United States of America in 2023
by the South Carolina United Methodist Advocate Press.

Library of Congress Cataloging-in-Publication Data
People of My Journey
p. cm.

Cover photo: choochart choochaikupt

ISBN 979-8-9851495-9-3

*I dedicate this book to my late parents,
Henry Hardin Holt and Caroline Cannon Holt,
who were the finest examples of Christian faith I ever witnessed.*

Table of Contents

Introduction 7
Evelyn Bell 9
David Wingo 11
Great-Great-Uncle DJ Fant 15
Penny's Family 17
Rainbo Breadmen 19
Hal and Mary 23
"Enoch Walked with God" 27
Henry Thomson 29
Willie Lee Buffington 31
Gary Crawford 35
Dot Crouch 39
Joe Lester Allen 41
Helen Derrick 43
Granny Mack 45
Sam Crouch Sr. 47
Jimmy and Hilda Bolt 51
Wally Brock 53
Thomas Evatt 55
The Mount Holly Trinity 57
Gene and Margaret Simpson 61
Perry 63
Ann Mayfield 65
Mary Hayes 67
Bill Crotzer 69

Mentors:
The Rev. Dr. Ed Ellis 73
The Rev. Adger McKay 77
Dr. John Benjamin Bedenbaugh 81
The Rev. Julian Lazar 85
The Rev. Dr. Jim Nates 89
How I Became a Marginal Preacher 93
The Residency Rebels 95
The Rev. Douglas Arthur Bowling 97

Grand Finale 101
About the Author 103

Introduction

Back when I was in high school in the late 1960s, a Sunday school teacher told the class, "You will be the same person in five years as you are today except for the people you meet and the books you read." It is certainly true that my life has been shaped by my relationships and my educational experience.

My life has been all about people—my family, my friends, and the members of the churches I was appointed to as pastor. These relationships have deepened my faith in God and shaped my life for the better.

Some of those relationships go way back to my childhood. Some of my best lessons about the power of God's love and grace were given to me long before I went to seminary. Of course, my parents were the greatest influences on my life; parents usually are. But I will save those stories for another day and perhaps a later book.

I am a "grace preacher," meaning I preach a lot about God's love and forgiveness. It is also important for people to behave in Christlike ways. But I have always believed that once people know how much they are loved, they will respond in loving obedience to God. My stories will illustrate this point and emphasize the power of love and grace.

So here are some stories about people that have helped make me who I am today.

—The Rev. Arthur Holt
March 2023

Evelyn Bell

I hated school! I hated it so much so I tried to run away several times during the first grade.

The person who turned things around for me was Evelyn Bell, my third-grade teacher at Whitney Elementary School. Mrs. Bell was a soft-spoken lady who never raised her voice in anger or discipline; in that way she was a lot like my mother. Some teachers berate the students who misbehave, but not Mrs. Bell. She seemed genuinely concerned and interested in all of us.

There was a boy in our class, I'll call him Mark, who was often getting into trouble for stealing things, especially baseball gloves. One day when we returned to the classroom after a recess period, Principal J.Y. Wallace came into our classroom accompanied by an older boy.

"Now, which boy did you see holding your glove?" the principal inquired.

The boy pointed to Mark, and when Mr. Wallace looked inside Mark's desk, sure enough, there was the glove.

When Mark left with the principal for yet another paddling (or as we students used to say, "for another meeting with the board of education"), Mrs. Bell put her math book down.

She said, "Students, Mark wants a baseball glove so very badly, but I don't think his folks can get him one right now."

She was right. Mark's often dirty and tattered clothing suggested he came from a very poor family. I seem to remember someone saying he was being raised by his grandmother.

Then Mrs. Bell continued, "We ought to get him one."

Her plan, apparently devised right there on the spot, was for us to collect Top Value stamps, those yellow stamps grocery stores gave to reward their customers. Every dollar spent was rewarded by one yellow stamp, and a book containing hundreds of stamps could be redeemed for really nice things like lamps, luggage, toys, or baseball gloves. Mrs. Bell asked us not to tell Mark anything about our plan but to ask our parents for their help.

In a few weeks, we managed to collect enough stamp books to get Mark a glove. The anticipated day finally came; Mark was summoned to the front of the class. Most of the times when Mark was called up to Mrs. Bell's desk, it was to be presented with another note to take to the office, a note entitling him to another paddling.

Mrs. Bell handed him a neatly wrapped box, saying to him, "Mark, your friends decided to get you a present."

I'll never forget the look on his face as he opened the box and saw the glove. He didn't show happiness or surprise. It was more the look of doubt and uncertainty. Perhaps he wondered if it was a cruel joke or some kind of taunting.

"It really is yours to keep," Mrs. Bell reassured him.

Mark and I were in the same schools for the next five or six years, and I never heard of another instance where he was accused of stealing anything ever again.

I don't remember what we read that year. I have forgotten what we studied in science and math. But I will never forget the lesson Mrs. Bell taught us about grace, how sometimes you can change a life with love when paddlings have failed. In her own quiet way, Mrs. Bell exemplified God's grace and changed the life of one troubled boy forever.

That lesson wasn't wasted on me, either.

David Wingo

Many of us suffered at the hands of bullies in our early years. I was a sixth grader when I had my taste of bullying, and I know the best way to solve that social problem: Be fortunate enough to have a brave classmate take a stand against the bullies, and they will often back down. But it takes a special, brave friend, one who is willing to risk his or her own reputation for you.

David and I had been in every grade together since we began first grade, but we were not close friends. I loved team sports like baseball, football, and basketball. David didn't often join in our recess games. Instead, he walked down by the creek, looking for frogs and fish. He talked about his father's tractor and farm animals. We all liked David, but he didn't mix with us much.

My sixth-grade year was a tough one. My grandfather had died as school began and my family was planning to move across town to live with our grandmother. I discovered that I needed glasses, and glasses were not cool! Word got out that I had a girlfriend who lived in our neighborhood; it was widely rumored that we even played together (she was a great baseball player). My buddies still believed girls were to be avoided—funny how that changed the next year. And I liked to sing, plus I took piano lessons.

There was a meeting held one day during lunch, and a group of boys decided some of us were sissies. Glasses plus girlfriend plus music landed me in that group. These macho boys made our lives miserable with their taunting, and the one thing that hurt worse than anything was when my best friend turned on me. He had always chosen me first when teams were being arranged for our recess games. Now neither team captain chose me until last. I was good enough to be a first-round draft choice any day!

My friends and I tried the "ignore them and they will go away" tactic for a few days without success. Although I was smaller than many of the boys, I began to react to them with hostility. One time during a recess touch-football game, one of the bullies decided he was going to run with the ball—right over me. He lowered his head, stuck his arm out in front of him, and charged right toward me. I knew I was about to be knocked down, but I also knew if I hit him from the side instead of head-on, I could probably knock him down a bank, maybe even into the creek. It worked perfectly. I will never forget the surprised look on his face as he hit the soggy soil at the edge of the creek. That sure felt good.

Fall passed, winter came, and the taunting continued. Besides making me hostile, the teasing was having an effect on me. I was beginning to believe it. I must be less manly than the others. I couldn't seem to play ball as well as I used to.

Our classroom was in an old two-room building set apart from the rest of the school, a building that had been a mill office and a barber shop in earlier incarnations. The door didn't shut well, especially when blasted by a strong north wind, and so the teacher assigned two of us—David and me—to sit right by the door in order to close it quickly when it blew open. Even with this close seating arrangement, I didn't become David's friend. Perhaps that is why his courageous actions have always puzzled me. He did what he did because it was the right thing to do, not because he considered me his friend.

One day as we returned to class from recess, the taunting began again. Our teacher was on the way but not in the room yet, and so there were no curbs on the abuse.

As four or five taunters gathered around my desk, David quietly took command: "That is the stupidest thing y'all are doing to Arthur. How long are you all planning to keep up this stupid game? I wish you'd stop it right now—or else start calling me a sissy, too!"

I had been staring at the floor, but I looked up in time to see the boys go to their seats in total shock and disbelief. Someone had dared to call their actions "stupid," and they knew it was the truth. They looked as if someone had physically slapped them. The teasing stopped almost immediately.

I don't think I even said thanks to David. I, too, was in shock that he had taken such a heroic stand. He was willing to be "numbered with the transgressors"—with me—to stand with me in shame if that would stop the teasing (and you can see how this story has found its way into my sermons).

Even after his heroic act, I did not become David's close friend. It was years later that the significance of David's actions on my life became clear to me, and now I wonder what might have happened if he hadn't had the courage to challenge evil in that mini-society.

A few years ago, I read the obituary in the Spartanburg Herald newspaper for David's father. The graveside service was to be in the middle of a hot afternoon, but I knew I had to go. I didn't recognize David after forty years, and so I had to ask a family member which one was David. I walked over to him, and he called my name immediately. I gave him the long overdue thanks he deserved, and he brushed it off like it was nothing.

"Believe me, it was something," I told him.

Next I went over to David's elderly mother and introduced myself to her, and she said, "I remember you." I told her that when we were in Whitney School together, her son David had been a very good boy. She smiled, and sounding like our mothers, she responded, "Sometimes."

I laughed and replied, "No ma'am. All the time."

Note: I have discovered David's great-great-great-great-great-grandfather William Wingo, my great-great-great-grandfather Claiborne Holt, and my great-great-great-great-grandfather Ellis Cannon all served together in the Virginia Line during the Revolutionary War, and that they and others in their regiment moved to Spartanburg at the same time. William Wingo was also present at the Siege of Savannah on October 9, 1779, when my great-great-great-great-grandfather Reuben Holt was killed. Small world!

Great-Great-Uncle DJ Fant

My grandfather Cannon died in August 1961. In a matter of a few weeks, my grandmother decided she did not want to move away from the beautiful three-acre home on Spartanburg's east side that she and Granddaddy had built fifteen years earlier. She quickly designed a four-room apartment that attached to the far end of the large screened porch of the original six-room house. By December 28, 1961 that apartment had been built, and my sister, our parents, and I moved over to the older dwelling.

Living in the same complex with my grandmother meant I got to visit more often with uncles and cousins who often came to see her. Probably the oldest visitor was my granddaddy's ninety-three-year-old uncle DJ Fant, a Southern Railway engineer. Having determined to be a better man after the death of one of his children around the turn of the century, Uncle DJ had become a well-known Christian and Missionary Alliance evangelist who combined his passion for his train with his devotion to his faith.

Uncle DJ was the great-grandson of Revolutionary War hero Major Joseph McJunkin, and he was very fond of my joke-telling grandfather (his nephew) that he lovingly called "my boy."

When I was twelve years old, Uncle DJ came for a visit, and so I went out on the porch to visit with him. He was in mid-sentence in a story when his head abruptly fell forward and he became unconscious. I went into the house and reported to my mother that Uncle DJ had just died!

She told me he'd only fallen asleep and that I should return to my seat to wait for him to wake up, which he did about ten minutes later. He resumed his story exactly where he had left off, as if he hadn't missed a beat. On that visit, he was promoting a program that was encouraging people to read the Bible from cover to cover. It was called "Read It Through in '62." I doubt I did, but I sure remember the slogan!

Uncle DJ had two terminals to his routine train route. One was in Greenville,

South Carolina, and the other was Atlanta. At each terminal, people frequently showed up to see his unique train and to hear a short sermon as he exited the train. The attraction of the train was that he had replaced the "cow-catcher" with a brass plate shaped like an open Bible bearing the Scripture, "Thy Word Is Truth."

One of the stories I read about him was that one time his train was robbed of a load of gold. After the men were apprehended, Uncle DJ went to the prison to visit the robbers who had threatened his life, repaying them by getting down on his knees and praying for them.

Another fascinating aspect of Uncle DJ's story is he was happy to be a colorful train engineer whose high speed and exploits were the stuff songs were made of. He always blew the train whistle as he passed his friends' houses to remind them he was praying for them. But except for the cow-catcher Bible, there was nothing about his faith that was showy.

Toccoa Falls Bible Institute presented him with an honorary degree. When they put the hood over his head, he was heard quite loudly muttering, "Worldly trappings!"

Uncle DJ died a few years after our porch conversation. I remember reading in the paper that one week before he died, he had participated in the groundbreaking for a new Christian and Missionary Alliance Church in the Atlanta area.

Since my grandfather had such a big influence on my faith development, it was nice to have known his uncle who had inspired his faith! My grandfather often said, "I was called to preach, and my sons answered that call."

His grandson did, too!

Penny's Family

On Christmas Day 1971, I made an eventful trip from Spartanburg to Blacksburg, Virginia, to have Christmas dinner with my new girlfriend and her family. I borrowed my parents' car, and the fact that it was totally lacking heat must have been a passive aggressive statement from my parents and sister that they were not totally happy with my decision to desert our annual family gathering.

If you were a student at women-only Converse College back in the 1960s, your dating opportunities were somewhat limited to the predominantly male Wofford College, located one mile away. If you further limited your dates to a particular subset of Wofford students (like those who went to church on Sunday mornings), your gene pool was extremely limited. Therefore, all of the guys Penny dated were my closest friends.

So when they heard I was making this pilgrimage to Virginia, they all rallied around me to warn me of the fate that awaited me. Penny, they said, was well-guarded by her divorced mother and a widowed grandmother. I'd better be on my best behavior, they laughingly said, because they knew I was never on my best behavior. Penny's sister had gotten married six months earlier, and her new husband warned me that if Penny and I were considering a future life together, we should keep this fact to ourselves unless we wanted to experience the Spanish inquisition firsthand.

With this preparation in mind, I drove the six hours, arriving right on time for the one p.m. Christmas dinner. Attending the festivities in addition to "Mom" and "Gaga" were Penny's two uncles and two aunts, plus her four cousins, three boys and one girl ranging from six to eleven years old. I was seated across from a nearly deaf, very feeble lady who looked about eighty-five years old, old enough to be Penny's grandmother, and so I played nice to her all day, especially when I saw her reach out and violently snatch a toy away from Penny's uncle. (OK, it was one of those very annoying "Newton's Cradle" perpetual motion toys, five steel balls suspended from strings that keep swinging for hours, but still she struck fear into my heart and made me tighten up on my behavior.) Then she kept asking me who I was going to vote for in 1972, and when I said "Nixon," to my great surprise she seemed genuinely disappointed.

The rest of the family was just delightful, especially a lady I assumed was Penny's Great-Aunt Elizabeth who looked to be maybe seventy and was so very sweet. Imagine my surprise to learn the spry seventy-year-old lady was almost eighty and was actually Penny's grandmother, and that the perpetual motion toy thief was Gaga's younger sister. Think of all that charm I had wasted on the wrong person!

I didn't realize I was the fourth "new boyfriend" Penny had brought to Christmas dinner in the past four years, and so at the end of the dinner when I told everyone I had enjoyed being with them and I looked forward to being with them next year, they all laughed, and I didn't understand why. I was just the latest float in the parade.

I did go back for a second Christmas, and then a third, and then about twenty more before this tradition ended. But that first Christmas, after I had already fallen in love with Penny, I fell in love with her family.

Rainbo Breadmen

"Martha" is not a nickname I'm particularly proud of ever having, but there is an interesting story behind it.

In 1974, my wife, Penny, and I were living near Roanoke on Bent Mountain on a farm recently purchased by her Aunt Sue and Uncle Frank. Sue invited us to live there so there would be someone to take care of their horses, and she also knew I needed some time to figure out what I was going to choose as a career. The previous two years had been spent in youth work in Lyman, and my work there had not been entirely successful, to say the least. There is nothing like a total absence of training to ensure great lack of success and unhappiness.

So after two years of struggle and depression, I needed to decide about seminary or choose some other direction for my life. Sue and Frank generously gave me a place to think things through, and it surely seemed to be God's will for me at that point.

My first job there was with DeBondt Insurance Agency out of Charlottesville. Francis DeBondt sent me to the Blacksburg area to sell disability policies to the faculties of then-Virginia Polytechnic Institute and Radford University. I did very well for a couple of months in spite of very little training (again), but then I ran out of leads at those universities and it was time to turn to traditional insurance selling. I was miserable. I switched to a Prudential agency, but I was no more successful there, because by then I was too depressed and defeated to make myself telephone and visit total strangers. So in January I worked for a temporary agency for several weeks before I decided to try a new career in the bread delivery business.

Rainbo Bread had a huge bakery and distribution center in downtown Roanoke. Why I thought I would like this job is beyond me, but I was desperate by then. I filled out a job application and then had an interview with the sales manager, a guy named Wayne Semones. The drivers at Rainbo called him "Sea-Moans." When he told me his name, it sounded like he pronounced it "Ter-moan-ez." When I repeated it, he was not impressed with my pronunciation—a good start to any interview process! His pronunciation was because of the dental partial he wore in place of his front teeth. I later learned that his dental situation was connected with some interesting breadman folklore. A few years earlier, there had been a bread war during which breadmen actually fought one another and enjoyed smashing each other's cakes, pies, and bread on store shelves. A driver of a competitive bread company drove his truck at fifteen mph very close to Wayne and stuck his fist out as he passed him, knocking Wayne and his front teeth out cold!

Sea-Moans looked at my application: a Bachelor of Arts in religion, several jobs in churches as youth director, and a few months in insurance. He wasn't impressed. He had several reservations about me, the most accurate one being that a person with a college degree didn't last long in the bread business. But those who did persevere would advance in the company, he said.

With that, he announced there were no job openings at this time but that he would keep my application on file. Perhaps another concern was my hair. It was long! This was the early 1970s, and lots of us had long hair back then. But this did not give a person a good chance at being employed by companies still being run by the older generation.

I thanked Wayne for his time, and got up to leave his office. As we entered the hall, we ran into a man in his sixties. What hair he had was gray and very short, and judging by all the smiles and uncomfortable laughs from everyone around him, I knew that he was a big boss. It turned out he was THE big boss, Walter Earl Ruble.

Caught by surprise, Sea-Moans mentioned that I had applied for a job and then he asked me to introduce myself to the boss, and so I extended my right hand and said, "Hello. I'm Arthur Holt."

Mr. Ruble took one look at me and said, "Martha Who?" and he and everyone laughed.

I laughed also, and then I said, "Well, I guess it is high time for that haircut!"

Again Mr. Ruble laughed, and then he turned and whispered something to Sea-Moans before he left the hall. As I was walking toward the exit, Wayne called to me, inviting me back into his office. He was still laughing in amusement at what had happened, and then he announced, "Mr. Ruble liked the way you handled yourself in the hall. He thinks you will do well with our customers. He said that if you get a haircut, you've got a job."

I guess I ought to thank my Grandfather Cannon and Daddy for giving me their quirky sense of humor.

I next learned about another reservation Wayne had about me: "Some of these truck drivers are rough and tough guys who use rough language and won't take kindly to someone preaching at them."

I assured him that while my work in churches and my faith were important to me, I wasn't one who was pushy about my faith, nor was I someone who is easily offended by rough language. With that, Wayne welcomed me and took me downstairs to the room where the bread salesmen were returning from their deliveries, tallying their orders, and turning in money received.

And then he hung that nickname on me, "Guys, this is Martha. After he gets a haircut, he's going to start working with you tomorrow." I don't think they ever bothered to learn my name! I was Martha for as long as I was there.

One day, Penny came to pick me up after work. As each salesmen walked toward his car, Penny would ask them if Arthur was still there in the building. None of them had any idea who she was talking about. Finally, she uttered the name she had vowed never to call her husband as she asked one guy, "Is Martha still in the building?" He answered, "Oh, yeah, she's still in there."

Every morning I was up at five a.m. I tossed some hay to the horses and drove forty-five minutes from our mountain home to the bakery. When it snowed, that trip became a journey. I still remember the look on one driver's face when I passed his approaching car while traveling sideways! My headlights clearly showed the fear in his eyes.

Most days I was getting home after five p.m. After eating supper with Penny, I hit the bed.

I really enjoyed my work at Rainbo Bread. There was a loyalty between the salesmen that could teach lots of churches how brothers and sisters in Christ ought to stand by each other. They helped each other even if the recipient of the help wasn't very popular. They just did this because that was how coworkers were supposed to act.

And they used humor to deflect serious problems whenever they could. One of them suggested my company-provided uniform needed alteration. "Your pants look like a family moved out of the back of them. Here—put two loaves of bread back there!" When a big bolt was found inside a hoagie bun at Virginia Tech where Penny's mother was the dining hall manager, one of the managers in the bakery said, "Tell your mother-in-law that those hoagie buns are so big that we have to put bolts in them to hold them together." A trainer named David rode with me one day, and at noon he asked me when I stopped for lunch. "After I finish the route," I answered. "Diabetics have to eat sooner than that," he replied, and so I pulled into a burger joint. Over lunch, I said, "I didn't know you had diabetes." He replied, "I don't."

The breadmen were also very fond of giving each other nicknames to build strong bonds of care between one another. I was Martha. My trainer was "Mennix." His real name was Dennis but his nickname was a cross between Dennis the Menace and Mannix, a popular TV character in that day. Mennix and Sea-Moans made sure

I was well-trained for my job. They prepared me for about any surprise—except for the odd assortment of characters who worked the city market at eight a.m. each day. I saw a number of cross-dressers and streetwalkers there.

I probably would have stayed at Rainbo Bread if it hadn't been for an offer I received from Julian Lazar to come to Irmo to work with him at Union Church while I began my studies at the Lutheran Seminary. It was a difficult thing to turn in my resignation to Mennix and Sea-Moans.

But they got the last laugh—they decided to throw me to the wolves. My last week, I was given a route I had never driven, covering for the vacationing Leo, a twenty-five-year veteran driver. It took me an hour longer that Leo to run that route, causing the guys to kid me about being so much slower than an old man.

I answered their taunts by changing a few of the words of the number one song of that year: "I'm not Leo. My name is Martha. Leo left you a week ago. My eyes are not brown, but mine won't leave you till I've finished his crazy route."

Those two jobs—selling insurance and driving a bread truck—prepared me quite well for my future as a pastor. I got more comfortable with meeting total strangers and saw the value in Christian fellowship. Churches would do well to follow the example of breadmen helping one another even if they didn't particularly like the person they helped.

But there was one big difference between the world of breadmen and life in the church. In the bread world, "ascend" did not mean to go up; rather, it was what they called the back end of the truck.

Hal and Mary

When Penny and I decided to move back to South Carolina from Bent Mountain so I could prepare for the ordained ministry (and you can still see her black heel marks all along I-77), we were soon adopted by members of the church staff—secretary and organist Mary Bonnett and her choir director husband, Hal.

Hal and Mary had three married daughters our age, so they didn't need to adopt us, but they did anyway. This adoption meant frequent meals together (even midnight waffles) and a place to survive when ice storms wiped out the power in Irmo. We spent a week camped out by the fire in their living room on one such occasion and even went to Disney World together once. What Hal and Mary meant to us cannot be overstated. They became our family there in Irmo.

Mary was a fantastic secretary, but she was perpetually late to work by twenty minutes. She always stayed overtime by at least an hour a day. This tardiness didn't bother anyone but our business administrator, but he finally surrendered. People tended to congregate in front of Mary's desk because she was so much fun to visit with. One day I was standing by her desk when Mary put a call on hold and said in a much-exaggerated Southern accent, "Ahh-thah, there is a nice Southern lady on line one who wants to speak with Ahh-thah."

I picked up the phone on her desk and said, "Hello... Oh, hi, Mom!" Mary was mortified! But the group around her desk had a good laugh at her expense.

Trying to accurately type the weekly bulletin was difficult for Mary, mainly because of the constant phone interruptions and people coming into her office. Therefore, her bulletin typos were always very entertaining. Quite memorable was an anthem title based on Psalm 84 that Mary mistyped as "How Lovely are Thy Swellings, O Lord." Senior Pastor Jim Nates didn't notice that until it was time for the anthem (right before his sermon), and he could barely continue with the service!

Hal was the choir director for the Chancel Choir as well as the Youth Choir. The church was exploding with new members in this era, growing from a few hundred to a few thousand members in one decade. The Staff-Parish Relations Committee had been hoping to hire a full-time music director (with a music degree) as soon as finances would allow this, and during my first year in Irmo this was accomplished—rather suddenly.

It blindsided many of us who were Hal's close friends and choir members, creating a good bit of anger among us. What could have been a powder keg was diffused by Hal, who was always completely supportive of whatever his church chose to do. He warmly welcomed his replacement, remained as a member of the choir, and told us all he was in full agreement with the decision to hire a full-time person. What an example of Christianity he was—in this and so many other instances.

Being freed of some of his Sunday duties, Hal took on a new duty without being asked. We had three back-to-back worship services beginning at eight-thirty and ending at high noon every Sunday. This was exhausting for us worship leaders and especially to us pastors, so Hal prepared fresh coffee for us to grab in the ten-minute breaks between services. Then he would hold hands with us and say a prayer for us, sending us back out renewed by caffeine and the Spirit.

Sincere, loving Christian people are often watched and admired without ever being aware of it. This was certainly true of Hal and Mary. Their phone rang one day. It was a neighbor who said, "Mary, could you please come over to talk with me? I am really struggling with my faith right now, and I think you can help me."

Mary felt overwhelmed, asking, "Wouldn't you rather I ask our pastor to come by to see you?"

"No, Mary," the neighbor replied. "For years I have watched you get your three little girls up and out the door for church every Sunday. If you can't help me, no one can."

I was there at Union United Methodist Church in Irmo from May 1975 until February 1981, six wonderful years. A huge reason those years were so wonderful was that Hal and Mary were such a big part of our lives. When we moved to Saluda, South Carolina, our meeting places became restaurants halfway between our homes. And when our babies' due dates arrived and the contractions began, we headed the forty miles from our home to the Bonnetts' to wait for the time when Penny would be admitted to the Lexington County Hospital.

Mary had a lengthy battle with breast cancer that began the summer we first arrived in Irmo, and the cancer finally took her life a few years after we moved away. But talk about a fighter. Mary refused to surrender to the cancer, electing to have back surgery so she could remain mobile for travel, and travel she did until shortly before her death.

Hal remarried later, and to our amazement his second wife looked very much like

Mary (even though her name was Jane). He moved over to Jane's home in Winnsboro, South Carolina, and continued his active work with church choirs and his chapter of the Barbershop Quartet.

His death closed a very significant chapter in our lives, one for which Penny and I will always be thankful.

"Enoch Walked with God"

At the Christmas gathering of the Columbia District pastors and spouses in the mid-1970s, a baldheaded older pastor named Enoch Finklea read a sermon parody written by one of his seminary professors. In that "sermon," the writer performed a detailed examination of each line of the poem, "'Twas the Night before Christmas," looking for hidden meanings in every line much like we preachers dig deeply into a text of scripture.

One of the lines I remember is the line "he turned with a jerk"—it was interpreted to mean Santa had a helper of low repute! I knew someday I had to get a copy of it, and I had to get to know that pastor.

A few months later, our district pastors went to Asbury Hills Camp for a retreat. There was another pastor in attendance who wore a toupee. Both he and Enoch left the meeting room for a moment, and when they returned, Enoch was the one wearing the toupee! It took us all a moment to figure out what had changed. Again I said, "I have to get to know this pastor!"

Enoch was a beloved pastor. Most of us move every few years to a new congregation. But Enoch stayed in the Pelion, South Carolina, area for most of his ministry, serving four churches for several decades. One of the benefits for Enoch was that the churches allowed—even encouraged—him to preach revivals all over the South. I doubt any other South Carolina United Methodist pastor has preached in more churches than Enoch did.

Those revivals were as unique as Enoch was. For one thing, Enoch bought every tacky trinket he could find at flea markets—crosses, small pocket knives, tiny flashlights, candy—in large volumes and handed these out to those who attended his revivals. But those things had a way of conveying Enoch's joy and love and opening people's hearts to receive his message. There was nothing quite like looking out on a congregation where everyone was chomping on a lollipop.

His sermons were hilarious, and yet they tugged at everyone's hearts. He loved to tell about his first sermon—a time he preached everything he knew to say and then repeated it again until he saw a lady in the back pew beginning to cry. "I've got one," he thought. But after the service ended, the lady left without saying a word. Several years later when he was leaving that church, she asked him if he remembered his first sermon and the fact that she cried, adding, "Enoch, I cried because you were the most pathetic preacher I'd ever seen!"

Back in the 1990s, many churches had annual revivals, and whereas it was usual for crowds to begin rather large and then dwindle the rest of the week, Enoch's crowds grew larger every night. Sitting in the chancel area, I got to watch the expressions on the faces of the people. And those faces expressed enjoyment and happiness as they heard a message that spoke of God's love for them. When he closed the service with a song (during which you could hear his voice over everyone else's), he would invite people to come kneel in prayer, and the altar (as we call it) was always packed with people who felt they had been drawn closer to God that night.

Enoch seemed to always be thinking of others. He told me he and I were going to Walmart to get my wife a new iron after he heard her say her old one was shot. While there, he decided he needed a cola to drink. Seeing the waitress was all stressed out, he kept going up to the counter to order one thing after the other while chatting with her. When we finally left the canteen area, the waitress was smiling. That is what he thought was his duty as a Christian—to lift people up out of their stress and sadness.

When he was about fifty years old, Enoch had to have heart surgery to replace a damaged heart valve. He knew his wife, Mary, and dozens of their friends would be there at the hospital during the many hours of the surgery. Again thinking of others, Enoch arranged a dinner for twenty-five people to be brought into the waiting room at the hospital. While Enoch was unconscious with his chest opened up, his friends and family were dining on food Enoch had ordered for them, reminding them that while they were thinking and praying for him, he was remembering them in his love.

We were all thankful that he did well with the surgery and with the pig's valve placed in his heart. Of course, Enoch incorporated this story into his sermons, telling people that he had always loved ham. But now whenever he ate it, he felt a little guilty. He always felt like he was having a family reunion when he ate ham or barbeque.

You can have all of your hellfire and brimstone preachers. I'll take one loving preacher named Enoch Finklea whose sermons would melt the hardest, coldest hearts! Just how many people Enoch brought into God's Kingdom and how many people became preachers after having him as their pastor, I don't know. But I'm sure he filled up a corner of heaven like he packed all those pews during those revivals.

I never got a copy of that Christmas sermon from Enoch. But I did get it from Chad Davis, who was the Columbia District superintendent in the 1970s. I've used it many times, always giving my friend Enoch the credit for this masterpiece.

Henry Thomson

After six wonderful years as the associate pastor of huge Union United Methodist church in Irmo, I was moved in February, halfway through appointment year (that runs from June to June), to three churches in Saluda, South Carolina.

There were eight United Methodist churches circling Saluda. I had three of them, and another pastor had another three. Then two were big enough to exist on their own with their own pastors. Henry Thomson was the pastor of the county-seat church, St. Paul, in downtown Saluda. Though he was in no way my boss or supervisor, he was twenty-five years older than I was, and he took it upon himself to take us young pastors "under his wings."

The nearest hospital was thirty miles away in Greenwood, and that was the place most of our members went when such care was needed. Henry would call to see if I had any members to visit, and he would offer me a ride. Then we would grab a bite of lunch, usually at Wendy's. I told him we could fix our own lunches before we went to the hospital, but he would answer me by saying, "Not while I have one dollar in my pocket will I ever eat food that I cook for myself!"

These carpooling events became opportunities for him to help me adjust to missing all of my Irmo friends. He could tell I was having a hard time. "You are not there now. You are here in Saluda," he would often tell me to encourage me to turn loose of my connections to the past and bloom where I had been planted.

One time, Henry seemed to delight in my getting a stark reminder that we were no longer in Irmo. We were expecting our first baby, so the Thomsons gave us a baby shower. Of course, we invited some friends from Irmo, but none of them was able to attend such an event fifty miles away. Henry sat there, smiling at the hard lesson I had learned. Our bishops discourage us from trying to maintain close relationships in our previous churches. That is one of the hardest things about being an itinerant pastor.

Henry always managed to stay calm in a storm, and I really admired him for that. One of the games church members like to play with their pastors is "hide and seek" when they have to go to the hospital. They must really think we routinely get our information directly from the Almighty and, therefore, we will know when one of our members enters a hospital. If we don't come to visit them, they are often very angry.

One such occasion happened with "Mrs. Jones," a St. Paul member. After she was discharged from the hospital, she let it be known she was very angry that Henry had not visited her, and so Henry went by her home. Her greeting at the door told him a lot; it was icy. But she eventually invited him in.

After a brief exchange of pleasantries, Henry said, "Mrs. Jones, I understand that you have been in the hospital."

She said, "Yes," quickly turning her head away from Henry.

So then he said, "Did you tell your doctor that you were going to the hospital?"

At that question, Mrs. Jones blew up. "Of course I did! What kind of foolish question is that!" she replied.

Then in a manner that was distinctly Henry, he smiled and said, "Um hm. I guess you must have wanted him to come see you in the hospital."

Following a moment of silence while this comment sank in, she said, "I guess I could have called the church to let you know."

Henry replied, "If you had, I'd have been right there with you."

I tucked that good example of pastoral care into a corner of my brain for those times I might need it.

Like other excellent pastors I have known, Henry died way too early, succumbing to pancreatic cancer a few years after we both moved away from Saluda. I visited him in his last days and found what I expected—a man who was working courageously and diligently to prepare his family and his church for his approaching death.

Henry always knew where he was heading.

Willie Lee Buffington

"One of the three churches has been having a little trouble," my district superintendent, Chad Davis, understated as he was preparing me for my new appointment. What I later discovered was they had been having a small war! "There is a retired pastor named Buffington in the church," he continued, "but I'm not real sure about him." Chad finished the story, telling me about a time he had led an administrative board meeting at that church and hoped he could calm things down. It had taken him over an hour to get them to agree on the minutes of their last meeting. It was a highly charged meeting, to say the least. Willie Lee Buffington met Chad on the steps of the church as everyone was leaving the meeting, waving his walking cane in the air while shouting, "Mendacity! Utter mendacity!" Both Chad and I had to consult Noah Webster.

I remember my first Sunday at Gassaway Church. A hefty man in his seventies came down the aisle. His hair was gray; his long beard was gray. He propped his arms on his cane as he closed his eyes and listened to my sermon. The only times I noticed him smile was when I made a mistake—a mispronunciation, for example. That is when I learned he was still awake.

Willie Lee had been a professor at Paine College, a United Methodist-related institution in Augusta, Georgia. Race relations were still somewhat chilly in Saluda, South Carolina, in those days, and some of our folks seemed puzzled as to why Willie Lee would want to spend his lifetime teaching at a historically Black college. I wanted to know more about this man, even though I was afraid of him.

"Come pick me up tomorrow," he growled with his hoarse voice as we were leaving the worship service, "and I will show you where your members live."

The next day I went up the dirt road to what had been a school back in the 1940s but now was the home of the Rev. and Mrs. Buffington. We did, indeed, go by the home of about every church member, but I had a difficult time finding the homes a second time because Willie Lee preferred all the abandoned dirt roads to the paved streets. We rode by a house that had fallen in, but the chimney was still standing tall.

"Stop here," Willie Lee ordered. For the longest time he just stared out the window at the ruins. Finally he said, "That's where I discovered America. That's my Daddy's house."

My eyes saw destruction; his eyes saw the warmth and security of his childhood home.

What had happened, I wondered, that led him to the calling to be a college professor at a struggling institution that had been founded by the "Yankee" branch of the Methodist Church after the Civil War? His story is amazing. It was included in a book published fifty years ago, Lives that Inspire, by Beatrice Plumb, and if I hadn't found that book and persuaded a very humble Willie Lee to tell me his story, I might never have known about the giant of a saint who was becoming my friend.

When he was a young nine-year-old boy, Willie Lee was standing by his house, crying because someone had just stepped in the mud pie he was "baking." He was consoled by a Black man who was walking home from his job as the schoolteacher at the segregated school for Black children, which was located nearby. This Black man was named "Professor" Eury Simpkins, and he encouraged Willie Lee by saying, "Be a man! The world needs men!" That was the beginning of a friendship that would transform both the boy and the teacher.

In 1920, twelve-year-old Willie Lee had to quit school to help earn a living as his father's helper in a saw mill, but Professor Simpkins kept prodding him to finish school. A door opened for Willie Lee to attend the Martha Berry School in Rome, Georgia, and while he was there he received weekly letters from Simpkins, encouraging the young student to keep studying. Often there was a dollar bill in the letter—two-point-five percent of Simpkins' monthly salary!

"I had to find a way to pay him back," Willie Lee said.

His education was interrupted by an illness that sent him home, and it was from this defeat that a miracle was born.

Now back home, Willie Lee would often walk down to Simpkins' schoolhouse. It really bothered Willie Lee that there were no books for students to read at the school. He remembered all the books at the Berry School, many that had been donated. He also knew the story of how Mrs. Berry had asked Henry Ford for one of those dimes he was famous for giving to poor little boys. Mrs. Berry took that dime, bought some peanuts, and within two years she had established an endowment for her school based on the sale of peanuts.

Willie Lee had a dime, so he bought five two-cent stamps. Looking at his Sunday school lesson book, he wrote down the names and addresses of the authors. He wrote five of them a letter, asking each one to send his friends a book for their school "or else please send me another two-cent stamp so that I can write another letter."

Four of those letters must have ended up in the trash can, but one of the recipients appealed to his church for books. A few months after he had mailed the letters, Willie Lee received a letter advising him to expect a train boxcar full of books to be delivered to him shortly!

Now Simpkins and Buffington had a wonderful and new problem: Where would all these books be stored? The community decided to help Willie Lee build a log cabin library for those books. Happy ending!

Well, happy beginning, actually.

As word spread about the boy who, like David, had conquered a Goliath of a problem with one thin dime, more books were sent his way. Churches all across the nation rallied to his cause. His unusual missionary work occupied Willie Lee's young adult years and also his college days at Furman. More log cabin libraries in other communities in South Carolina and Georgia were built to house all the books that kept coming. In all, one hundred and thirty libraries were built—quite a return from a one-dime investment!

Whenever my sermon text is about Jesus feeding the multitude with five loaves of bread and two fish, I immediately think of Willie Lee and his dime.

Willie Lee eventually received a seminary degree, and at his graduation ceremony, Eury Simpkins was awarded an honorary degree for the inspiration he had given to Buffington. I am not sure why Willie Lee spent his whole life at Paine College, a White man teaching at a Black college during the dark days of segregation and Jim Crow, but I believe it was his attempt to repay Eury Simpkins for all the encouragement he had been given—to be the man Simpkins inspired him to be.

In time, my fear of Willie Lee left me, and my admiration for him grew. "How are you doing?" I would ask him, and his answer was always "Slow." He was always the teacher and I was his latest student.

His wife died suddenly, and I was called on to lead her funeral. He complimented me on my eulogy, and since I was young, not sure how to respond to a compliment about a funeral, I stammered, "Well, just doing my job." I could tell by the look on his face I had given the teacher the wrong answer.

He waited a week to confront me about this, but the next Sunday he put his cane in my face and said, "When you have just buried a man's wife, don't ever say 'I was just doing my job!'"

I replied, "I knew the minute I said it that it was the wrong thing to say," and we embraced as he wept.

Almost a decade later, I was called to his bedside in a hospital in Spartanburg where he was dying. He had lost about half his weight, but he still had his long hair and beard.

"How are you doing?" I asked. "Slow," he replied. Then he commanded, "You're the one I want to preach my funeral."

I did so a few weeks later, and I told his grandchildren all about the man who gave his last dime to Jesus and changed so many lives. They had never heard the story. They had no idea that Willie Lee Buffington was a miracle worker!

Gary Crawford

A young pastor who is out of seminary for two years and being assigned to his first appointment on his own at the ripe old age of thirty-one just might need loads of friends in his three churches to survive! It helps if they are a half-a-bubble off-center ... or a French fry short of a Happy Meal.

Gary Crawford fit that description very well. The only thing I never understood was how he won the heart of his bride, Mrs. Faye! She was, indeed, a very lovely and classy lady, but perhaps she needed a mate who would keep life from becoming too serious for her. Gary would have been that ticket.

Gary was a cattle rancher (like lots of folks in Saluda are), but he also worked for Milliken. He was a highly respected member of Shiloh United Methodist Church, serving on many committees because everybody respected his opinions ... and his way of keeping things fun. There was the time the church was considering remodeling or adding on to their building so the exterior bathrooms (plumbed and wired but still more like modern outhouses than bathrooms) could be moved indoors. Gary pointed out that the bathrooms were "single occupancy," and so the fact that they were neither heated nor cooled and there usually were mosquitoes and bugs in them kept people from overstaying their welcome. The church eventually remedied this situation.

At church meals, Gary loved picking on the children. He was missing half of his pointer finger on his right hand, the result of an unfortunate industrial accident. He would hold a biscuit in his right hand in a way that made it look like his finger was inside of the biscuit, and after taking a bite, he would yell, "I just bit my finger off!" It didn't take the kids long to figure out he was fooling with them. Whenever someone disagreed with him or corrected something he had said, he would ease the tension of the moment by saying, "Excuse my pardon."

But underneath his zany exterior was the faith and faithfulness of someone who dearly loved his church. One of the tensions within that church was a group that leaned in the direction of holiness or Pentecostalism and wanted to push our Methodist Church in that direction. One very interesting man, in their mindset, had left our church to start his own church. As people were added to the rolls of his new church, some of them had new ideas that the founder found disturbing, and so he left that church, moved a hundred yards down the highway, and he built yet another church. This happened two more times, and the fourth iteration was quite a lively and exciting place.

It was that fourth incarnation of the church that the group wanted us to become like, and they stayed after us to attend Sunday night services at that other church since we did not have a night service of our own. This "encouragement" was repeated over and over—at church council meetings, at church dinners, in Sunday school classes—over many months. Then something Gary said took the wind out of that movement: "You know, if that church down the road has so much to offer our church members, why don't we just shut our church down and all of us move down there?"

I don't think I heard another word about Church Number Four. Gary had made the point: We are very happy with our church as it is.

Another thing I remember about Gary was his common sense. My first year there, the church official board was debating their annual budget with everybody looking for something to cut. Then Gary pointed out that there was already more money in the checking account than the next year's budget called for. "You mean we can pay next year's obligations even if we never pass the plate once? I move we adopt the budget and go home."

We did.

There was another thing Gary told me that has stuck with me across the years, a word of faith and wisdom. It actually was something his father said to him: "Son, I don't want to see you hot for your faith in God one day and cold the next. Pick a pace you can keep every day of your life, and you stick with that pace." Gary knew consistency in our spiritual journey was the best witness to our commitment to Christ.

There were a few folks in the church who did not like my use of modern translations of the Bible. As the saying goes, "The King James Version was good enough for Jesus, and it is good enough for me." I knew my use of New Revised Standard Version, New International Version, and other translations would be brought up at the next council meeting, and Gary reminded me some of the folks in the church had a "streak of mean" in them. Sure enough, there was criticism over this. I explained I would be using the KJV every Advent and Christmas because there is no beating the poetic beauty of that translation of the Christmas story (plus modern translations talk about Mary's virginity using words that make me blush). But for most of the year I would be using modern translations because it is difficult for folks to understand the meaning of Elizabethan English words and phrases. I confessed I also had trouble understanding this archaic language.

That set one dear lady off, as she exclaimed, "I think that if someone has gone through four years of college and four years of seminary and still can't understand the King James Version, that it means that there is something spiritually wrong with them!"

As we left that meeting and walked toward our cars, Gary walked past me mumbling, "Streak of mean, I tell you."

The following Sunday I walked into church with Gary. He gave me a thumbs up sign, or so I thought. But then he corrected me. "I had to take a Valium this big before I could come to church this morning." Some days I knew what he meant!

Having our first child while we were living in Saluda was a very interesting experience. When my grandmother Holt was having her children at the turn of the twentieth century, it was the custom for the pregnant woman to withdraw from public events and hide herself in her home until after the birth of the baby. Our baby was being born in 1982, but sometimes in Saluda I felt like we were my grandmother's contemporaries. On a home visit with one elderly lady, she began talking with me, her pastor, about having babies, and she ended by saying, "I hope your wife has an easy time of it." And then she added, "I guess I shouldn't be talking with a man about this."

Penny and I experienced similar conversations with many people. Even Gary, who was not an elderly person, had lots of reservations about talking openly about our having a baby.

"When I was a boy, I looked up one day while playing in the yard to see old Dr. Wise drive up into our driveway. He went into the house and then came back outside and left after a few minutes, and after that Daddy came over to me to say, 'You have a baby brother!' That was the first I heard about another baby being expected in our home. People didn't talk about it back then," he concluded.

We were in a Lamaze class, preparing for what we hoped would be "natural childbirth" where the baby's father remains in the delivery room with the mother-to-be. This had been a growing trend in hospitals during the 1970s and had become the norm by the time we got around to helping populate the earth. Poor Gary was actually afraid for me to be in the birthing room.

"I heard about a guy who saw his baby born and he became impotent after that. And I heard another guy went crazy," he said.

I tried not to laugh as I assured Gary that I would be fine.

I believe that is about the time he told me about one of his own hospital stays, and it was classic Gary. He was admitted because of an ulcer, and the orderly came to his room to give him a routine enema.

Gary asked him, "An enema? What is that?"

The orderly instructed Gary to stand over in the shower area and he would do the rest.

Gary told me, "That orderly had a hose pipe and a bucket, and we went to poking at me with that hose pipe. Every time he poked, I dodged."

Finally the orderly said to him, "See here, Mr. Crawford. You got to stand still."

Gary replied, "Huh uh! As careless as you are with that thing, there's no telling where you might stick that hose."

Gary, Faye, Penny, and I would go out often to meals—usually for steaks. Many times after the meals, I would see Gary reach for baking soda to calm his indigestion. One evening three years after we had moved to Edgefield, Gary reached for baking soda and then died of a heart attack. That made me wonder if he had been ignoring serious heart pains for years, thinking it was only indigestion.

Faye was devastated, as was Shiloh Church. And I lost one of the wisest, funniest friends I ever had.

Dot Crouch

At Gassaway United Methodist Church, I met a couple in their fifties who were very active in the church. Dot always sat on the front pew, and she always looked lifeless and stoic. I soon learned she and Thomas had lost their only child, Tommy, when he was twelve to leukemia. Most of Dot had died that day, although she insisted the death had been God's will. I tried at first to change her mind about this, but I soon learned the belief, that it was God's will, was the only way Dot could accept it and continue to live. This gave some meaning to his death.

I've always been one who attempts to show love by means of playful joking with people. It is always risky, but sometimes it pays huge dividends—as it did with Dot. One Sunday morning I announced that Drew University was asking for churches to look in their attics and basements for old historical items that could be sent to their archives center, and I suggested that we send Dot. I looked at her and noticed a crack in her stony face, an ever-so-slight smile! She had understood the love I was conveying via humor. From that day on, it was "on" between Dot and me as we each tried to out-kid the other.

One day when I was holding my infant daughter, someone said, "I wish you'd look at how much that baby looks like her daddy." Before I could acknowledge this comment, I heard Dot exclaim, "Oh! Let's pray for her. Maybe she will outgrow this. God can still work miracles, you know." She had struck back at me, and I sensed the love being conveyed in her awakening humor.

Then there was that covered dish dinner when someone commented on the fact that Dot always went everywhere with her husband, Thomas. When he took off in his truck, there was Dot going with him.

"I know why that is," I said. "That way Thomas never has to kiss her goodbye!"

Dot still sat on the front pew every Sunday, but there was life about her now. She had a smile on her face and was always ready to give a friendly greeting to those she met at church. But what really amazed me was the time Thomas came by the parsonage to talk with me. I was packing to move to a new appointment after three years at Gassaway, and Thomas wanted to say a private farewell to me.

"I want to thank you so much for what you have done for Dot during your time as our pastor," he said. "Nobody has ever been able to bring Dot out like you have—not since Tommy died."

A year later I learned Thomas was to be assigned as a "local pastor." In our denomination, a local pastor was someone who, usually later in life, feels a call to become a pastor. Under the guidance of a mentor and a district superintendent, these persons serve a small membership church. At retirement age, Dot and Thomas set out on a new career, ministering to congregations hundreds of miles from their home.

Occasionally I would see them, and every time Dot would ask to see a picture of my daughter. And each time she looked at the picture, she would exclaim, "Praise the Lord! She outgrew your looks!"

Joe Lester Allen

Joe Lester was my friend—maybe one of the closest I will ever have. Here I was, having completed eight years of education after high school. Joe Lester did finish high school ... barely. I had lived in two states already; Joe lived across the highway from his parents.

There are two reasons Joe Lester stands out as a special friend. First, he gave himself in genuine friendship to me like few others ever have. He wasn't after power or prestige or to get me to do him any special favors. He sensed I needed a friend. Second, Joe had received a death sentence—an autoimmune illness known as scleroderma that had forced him into retirement at age thirty-five and a disease that would end his life a few years later.

The way he used his limited days for others makes him an exemplary Christian in my book.

I became his pastor in 1981, or is that when he became my pastor? He seemed to be aware many people don't let pastors be human, and he was determined to let himself be one person I could be myself with. He kidded me about attractive ladies, saying, "I know you had to notice that one or else you're dead!" We swapped awkward teenage dating stories, but his always topped mine. "My buddy took me on a double date, getting me a date with this gal who had just broke up with her boyfriend after a three-year romance," Joe Lester drawled in his Lowcountry accent. "We didn't even get out of her driveway before she commenced kissin' on me! I was sitting in the back seat thinking 'Oh, Lord! Help me!'" He concluded a line he intended as a statement of his lack of sophistication: "The sad part, Arthur, is that I didn't have the sense to go back up there the next Saturday."

The first Holt child arrived in May 1982. It was November 1984 before she slept through the night! My wife and I took alternate nights getting up with the baby so neither of us became completely exhausted. Very few people in my three churches knew of our difficulty. Some who did see our fatigue were a bit critical.

"What would you have done if you'd had twins like I had," one lady said.

"I'd have frozen one of them and thawed her out in a year or two," I snapped back.

Somehow my friend Joe Lester knew, and he came by our parsonage to say, "Eliza and I have a feel for what you are going through. If we can help by taking care of the baby for a while so you can rest, let us know." That was Joe Lester, wanting to help, refusing to judge or criticize.

Sometimes when I drove the thirty miles to the nearest hospital, Joe Lester went along for the ride. The truth was that those sick folks were as glad to see Joe's round, smiling face as they were to see me.

During the last ten years of Joe's life, I moved three times. Joe was the only one from a former church who drove the many miles to come see me in each new church, and that says something about the caliber of his friendship.

Several years ago, I was invited back to Joe Lester's church for "homecoming." My return to my former church was bittersweet because Joe was now dead. His son was showing off a new six-month-old baby, and as I looked into the round face of that infant, I saw that Joe Lester was still among us in a new way.

Apparently I was not the only one who felt this world could use another Joe Lester in our midst! One day, I've got to tell that boy about his grandpa.

Helen Derrick

"Quick! Tell me what I believe!" said the frantic voice on the phone at my Saluda, South Carolina, parsonage in 1981. It was a member of one of my three churches, Miss Helen Derrick, a retired school teacher, choir member, Sunday school teacher, and a leader of our United Methodist Women.

Miss Helen always put her brother, her sister-in-law, and their children first, but her church was a very close second. She did all she could to get new members for Gassaway Church, and that usually meant inviting a new family to her house for a meal with her and her pastor and the pastor's wife. Humorous phone calls from her were always welcome.

"Miss Helen, what are you talking about?" I asked.

"The lady from Jehovah's Witnesses just left, and she's got me wondering what I believe and if I am right or wrong. She is such a nice visitor and so knowledgeable about her religion that she makes me feel right stupid," she answered.

Lucky for me, I had taken a course on "Major Sects" only a few years earlier at seminary, and so I went to find my notes before continuing our conversation. I quickly saw a couple of areas Miss Helen could engage her visitor in their next conversation. Most of the sects don't believe in the Trinity and they don't believe in the classical Protestant doctrine of salvation by faith alone. They believe that faith is important but not all-important. Good works, church attendance, evangelistic visits, and other good deeds must be added to faith if a person hopes to make it into heaven.

I suggested that she do reading on the Protestant doctrine of faith alone to be prepared for the next visit. She and I agreed these witnesses were doing something we all should be doing—making contacts to help her church grow. This would not be a confrontation but a good and meaningful conversation.

About a month later, this faithful Jehovah's Witness was back to see her prospect. As Helen listened to the witness's presentation, she heard her say, "And if I am good enough, I will be accepted into heaven."

Helen smiled and said, "Then you won't make it."

Her visitor didn't seem to understand the point of Miss Helen's comment, and so she continued with her presentation. Again she came to a point about some required good deed and said, "If I do this, then I will be in heaven."

Again, Miss Helen said, "Then you won't make it." The conversation continued until Helen interrupted her once again, saying, "You aren't going to make it."

This time the witness stopped and asked, "What are you saying? What are you trying to tell me?"

Miss Helen gave a short but complete explanation of our belief in salvation by faith alone, adding that if the lady was counting on her good works to get her into heaven, she would be disappointed. Our faith needs to be in Jesus, not in ourselves.

This member of the Jehovah's Witnesses was at a total loss as to what to say next.

"I haven't heard anything about this. I need to talk with my elders about this," she stammered, and on that note she left, quite confused.

The next time I saw Helen, she looked quite satisfied with her performance.

"Now I understand better what we believe," she proclaimed.

Granny Mack

One of my favorite friends in Saluda (in the Shiloh Church community) was Mrs. Willie "Granny" Mack, an active elderly lady whose spunk reminded me of Granny Clampett of the Beverly Hillbillies.

Granny Mack's skin was well-worn by the hours she had spent out in the broiling sun working in her garden, and she lived in a house whose wooden siding was also well-worn by years of baking sun and harsh weather. It had not had a paint job done on it in many years. Granny kept the highways hot with her old faded green and rusty pickup truck, and she often transported her blind brother to stores and doctor's appointments in it.

I remember one time when that old truck caught on fire! The flames shot up briefly through the floorboard before going out when the engine died, but the fire lasted long enough for Granny to reach across her brother's lap, open his door, and tell him to jump out, as she did also on her side.

Whenever she wanted a visit from me, she would call me to say she had made a pie or a cake, and there was a piece with my name on it if I would come by. Of course, I did. Her pies and her personality were both such treats.

I loved getting phone calls from Granny. She kept me abreast of all the news in that church community—who was in the hospital or sick at home—and she made my job much easier than if I had been left to read minds like most folks expect their pastor to do. But sometimes her calls were about other things. On many Fridays, I would meet my old boss, Jim Nates, at a tennis court located halfway between his house in Irmo and mine in Saluda. Then I would return home to cut the grass at the parsonage while still wearing my tennis attire.

One time she called late on a Friday afternoon to say, "Well, I drove home by your house today, and I told my son I had seen the preacher cutting his grass in his underwear."

I laughed and explained, "Granny, that was not my underwear. I was in my tennis shorts!"

She said, "It sure looked like your underwear to me!"

That comment, plus the time a female trucker blew the horn and whistled at me, caused me to change into blue jeans from then on before I cut grass.

When I moved to nearby Edgefield after three and a half years in Saluda, I still heard from Granny periodically. Once she called to tell me about the new pastor being assigned to her church a few years after I had moved.

"Son," she said, "We've been ruint! They done sent us a lady preacher."

I had heard who was to be appointed there, and the "lady preacher" was a good friend of mine and an excellent pastor, so I told Granny to hang in there. She was going to love her new pastor.

"I don't know, son. Granny will keep going to church. This is just a new idea I've got to think about."

Several months went by, and the phone rang again.

"Son, this is Granny. You can forget what I said about us being ruint because we were getting a lady preacher. We all love her."

I was happy to remind her I had told her so.

Granny Mack lived to be ninety-four years old. She had been widowed for fifty-seven years. (Some of you wives out there might say this was why Granny lived so long and why she was always so happy.)

Sam Crouch Sr.

I arrived in historic Edgefield, South Carolina, in June 1984. The church had recently rebuilt after a fire in 1981 that had destroyed the educational building and severely damaged the beautiful old sanctuary.

My predecessor, Dr. James Rogers, had decided to demonstrate the power of the Parable of the Talents, distributing thousands of his own dollars to the members of the congregation, asking them to use that money in ways that would not only return that loan to him but would also pay off the debt they owed for the repairs and new educational building. Six weeks later, the money was returned to the "master" and there were, indeed, sufficient funds for them to be debt-free by the time of my arrival. The Augusta Chronicle hailed Dr. Rogers as a miracle worker, and I thought to myself, "And I've got to follow this act?"

No one was sure of the cause of the fire, but it had occurred on the day the Rev. Jesse Jackson had been in town to encourage voter registration. Although it was never listed as the probable cause, arson was a possible cause. This suspicion was still strong when I arrived. At the same time, the citizens were about to elect a newly reorganized county council based upon the Supreme Court ruling, which broke the county up into single-member districts. The reason for this unanimous court ruling was that no Black candidate had ever been elected to public office in Edgefield County in spite of the fact that the county had been fifty percent Black and fifty percent White for many years.

I say all this to help the reader understand the climate I blindly walked into, not realizing the tensions present in the church and community.

Since the church had been consumed with rebuilding for the past three years, the greatest need the church had was for program planning. I asked about events planned to observe United Methodist "Special Days," like Women in the Pulpit Sunday to celebrate the ordination of women as pastors, which was fairly new back then.

Someone in town, not one of our members, let me know how some in the community felt about a woman's place when she asked me why it took so long for the church to rebuild after the fire.

I answered, "Well, everyone wanted to have their input into what was needed. The women wanted a modern kitchen, and—"

"The women?" she interrupted. "You all let women make decisions in your church?"

I said somewhat sarcastically, "Let them?"

I also wondered about a Special Day coming up in late September, "Continuing Journey Sunday," a day to celebrate our progress in South Carolina United Methodism since the merger of the formerly all-White annual conference and the formerly all-Black annual conference in 1972. Nothing was planned. Usually a Black pastor was invited into churches that were historically White and vice versa.

"What if I invite our former district superintendent who appointed me to Edgefield?" I asked the chair of our planning council.

"Great idea," he assured me.

So I invited the widely respected Dr. James Gadsden to preach.

If you have never lived in small-town America, you don't realize small towns have no need of telephone, telegraph, radio, or TV. The word gets out through blood connections.

Before I knew it, rumors ran wild. "The reason Arthur was appointed to our church was to integrate it!"

It didn't help me one bit when our bishop announced about that same time that he would be making cross-racial appointments in the future, and I was seen as a cog in this wheel of change.

One thing we pastors never want is to be run off, especially after only one year. I was quite frightened and caught totally by surprise. Dr. Gadsden had preached for me at my last appointment, twenty miles away, so I thought we had gotten beyond that impasse.

I began to hear that many of the members were planning to stay away from church that Sunday in protest. So I went to talk with Sam Crouch, the chair of our Pastor-Parish Relations Committee, who ran a hardware store in town. Sam had been chair of that committee for about twenty years, which is something that usually isn't allowed in Methodist churches. We believe in officer "rotation" so people don't get either burned out or too entrenched. I thought replacing him would be job one, but I am sure glad I didn't. Sam was in that position because everybody could trust him—pastors and parishioners. He always led all parties to make the right decisions, and his humility and calm demeanor were his greatest strengths.

Sam was also a real hero in race-relations in Edgefield, although you will never read of his behind-the-scenes work in any history book. Everybody shopped at

Crouch Hardware. It is the only place I remember ever seeing what the locals called "Thunder Jars" (large metal cans used as toilets in the homes of people who only had outhouses) for sale. He also chaired the school board, which had recently consolidated the two segregated high schools into one new integrated high school that they named in honor of the county's greatest living politician, Senator Strom Thurmond.

I went to Sam for help—everybody went to Sam for help. And Sam went to bat for me … or else I would have been a one-year pastor. Those who were upset at me were his good friends, and so he visited them and calmed their fears.

"Why is everyone so upset about the events of one Sunday, and why are they upset by our former superintendent coming back for a visit?" he asked them.

To one of his best friends, he joked, "I hope you are able to find an all-White corner of heaven!"

Meanwhile, I called my new district superintendent, the Rev. Sinclair Lewis, to let him know I was in over my head. He gave me some of the best advice I've ever been given: "Arthur, first win the battle going on inside of you. Then you will be able to take on the battle on the outside."

I followed that advice. I settled my innards. I had done nothing wrong or improper. We are a racially integrated denomination, and I had invited Dr. Gadsden for all the right reasons.

Then I went to visit my upset members.

A few of those members ranted and raved at me, but I remained calm.

"We have this day on our annual conference calendar, Continuing Journey Sunday, and I have always celebrated all of our conference's Special Days," I reasoned with them. "We observed that Special Day when I was in Saluda, and I thought all churches celebrated it. I am rather surprised your church has never observed it."

I think this helped. People began to see this wasn't just something their new pastor had pulled out of his sleeves.

The next Sunday, I made this same explanation from the pulpit. I concluded by saying, "If you feel you cannot be present that Sunday, I understand. But I hope you will be here! Dr. Gadsden is a great friend of this church. Here will be your chance to thank him for his hard work on your behalf."

My announcement seemed to be well-received.

Right after that, something else began happening. Those who were "immigrants" and not connected by bloodline to the older citizens had not really heard there was a problem at church. They started dropping by my office, one or two at a time, to apologize for how I was being treated.

"I'm glad you will understand if some members don't attend church that day," one angry member told me, "because I don't!"

Others came by to tell me they would be present for Dr. Gadsden's visit; some even changed their plans in order to be there. Other people whose attendance was somewhat haphazard decided to make sure they came that Sunday, even if they had missed Christmas and Easter. They said they wanted to send a message to the community that the church had moved on beyond old racial attitudes.

So on the Sunday Dr. Gadsden and his family visited, we had the largest attendance of any Sunday since I had arrived. And in the process, those members made a statement to me and to the entire membership: Arthur should get to stay as our pastor for as long as he so desires.

Several months later, our church held its charge conference, a special meeting of the official board conducted by our district superintendent. Present was Sinclair Lewis, and I will never forget his mini-sermon that he delivered to us in his Charlestonian brogue that day.

"You know, Christianity is hard for me," he preached. "It tells me I have to love some people I don't even like! I hope someday I can be in the same place spiritually that my mother is already. Anybody—man or woman, Black or White—could be her pastor today. Lots of us aren't there yet. But we've got to keep on growing."

I stayed there for three years. The church grew in numbers, especially in the number of young families and programs for those children. Our son was born there, and of all the places we have lived, this was one of my wife's favorites. It turned out to be a great appointment, and a lot of those previously upset people became my friends.

When the bishop decided to move me unexpectedly and without any warning in June 1987, one of those members who had stayed away from church on the day Dr. Gadsden preached asked me, "How can you justify leaving us so soon?"

Jimmy and Hilda Bolt

In 1987, I was appointed to Francis Asbury United Methodist Church in Greenville and moved there with my wife and two children. At a reception for us, I met an older couple, Hilda and Jimmy Bolt, both in their early eighties. I received from Jimmy the salutation that would become his usual greeting to me: "Good to know you, old boy!"

Hilda got right to the point: "I want you to get something started for our children," she said.

I thought she was another of those persons who was going to "delegate and disappear"—tell me what to do and then not offer to help. But I was wrong.

A few weeks later, we started a midweek program for the children: supper, choir, and classroom instruction. Jimmy and Hilda came, and when I expressed surprise at seeing them, Hilda responded, "You don't think I would ask you to do something and then not come to help you, do you?" That attitude alone would qualify a person as a saint in the eyes of most pastors.

Jimmy and Hilda came every Wednesday night and cooked the meal for the children for the next three or four years. But if we ever had a program for the children on Sunday afternoons, the Bolts were not available to help us because that was the time they spent visiting those who Jimmy called "the old folks" at a nursing home. Hilda played the piano for the residents while Jimmy distributed the hymn books. They couldn't seem to do enough to help others.

The first Christmas at the church I was told I had to meet the Bolts' great-grandsons, Jeff and Jay. I learned the Bolts had raised these boys, and I had to hear the story. When Hilda and Jimmy were in their early seventies, their granddaughter's marriage ended, and she was so devastated she was incapable of caring for her two preschool-aged sons. Family Court stepped in to find foster care for the boys.

When the Bolts heard about this, they went to the Family Court Judge to offer themselves as guardians.

"Not while I have one breath left in my body, Your Honor, will one of my descendants be put in the house of strangers," Jimmy said.

At first, the judge told them they were too old, but then he finally agreed to let the boys stay with their great-grandparents, at least for a little while. That stay lasted for about five years, during which time one boy began organ lessons from Hilda while the other boy developed an interest in medicine from retired pharmacist Jimmy. They were reunited with their mother for their teenage years, but they had received their directions in life from Jimmy and Hilda.

Today one boy is a doctor, and the other is a church organist and music teacher. It is easy to imagine their lives would have turned out very differently if Jimmy and Hilda hadn't stepped in.

Our church was struggling to survive. My wife, Penny, joined the choir to help it grow. Then she had to give it up because someone had to sit with our four-year-old son, John, who was now too old to stay in the nursery. Daughter Hillary was seven then. She sat quietly by herself on the front pew and never caused any problems—except for those few times when she made a sign for me to see, like the one that read, "Hurry up! I want to go home." John would not sit quietly by his sister, and so Penny planned to leave the choir.

"Old boy," Jimmy said, "let John sit with us. We will teach him how to behave in church."

I wondered how the Bolts, now eighty-five years old, would handle a squirming four-year-old boy, but John behaved better for them than he did for his mother and me. John would come home, talking about "Jimmy and Hilda" as if they were children his age. Three out of four Sundays my son sat with the Bolts; the fourth Sunday was the day Jimmy, Hilda, and John kept our nursery. After worship I would find Hilda, Jimmy, and John all sitting on the floor, playing with the babies.

"Old boy, look at what John built with blocks," Jimmy would say. "He's going to be an architect. Make sure he goes to college."

I promised that I would, but Jimmy must have doubted I would be able to keep that promise without some help. He and Hilda presented us with one hundred shares of stock in an electric utility company for John's education.

Methodist pastors move twice each decade on average, and it was our time to move in 1992. Hilda died about three years later, followed by Jimmy within a year. Both deaths were hard on John.

But the impact of these two saints upon my son's life showed in John's remark to me after I told him Jimmy had died.

"All I can say, Dad, is that somebody has got to step up and take his place in our world."

I knew that John was saying he would be that somebody.

Wally Brock

When I arrived at Francis Asbury UMC as their pastor in June 1987, I was welcomed as the church's savior. The church had been in decline for years, and most people blamed previous pastors for this decline. No pressure there.

It was common to hear that blame mentioned at social gatherings and meetings, and on one such occasion I noticed Wallace Brock grimace. The next day, Wally came to my office to tell me, "We ain't never had nothin' but good pastors. I liked them all." I told him this told me more about him than it did the pastors, and I knew I had a loyal friend in the making.

Wally was in his late fifties, I would guess. But he was disabled by a serious heart condition that had required triple bypass surgery. He might have completed a neighborhood elementary school but not much more. His accent and vocabulary told me a lot about Wally. He was pure backwoods country. In fact, if I had been filming "The Andy Griffith Show," I probably would have cast him as Earnest T. Bass.

Francis Asbury UMC had no greater evangelist than Wally. He would do anything to help, and every visitor received his personal invitation to return. Once I saw him talking with a neighbor over her trash cart and I teased him about talking trash with that lady. He laughed and said, "I was telling her she ought to come to our church." I have no doubt he was.

One of the programs we began in order to attract children and youth to our church was to join a basketball league. The church had once fielded great teams, and one pastor was renowned for having been thrown out of the gym by a referee! Someone suggested we could make a few bucks if we sold light refreshments—cokes, candy, popcorn, and hot dogs. Wally got all excited and volunteered to run the concession stand, which I named "The Brock of Ages Café." The name stuck.

A story I heard about Wallace as a young man is that he made a bet with a friend that for twenty-five cents he would marry "that girl over there," pointing at Thelma.

After only four months of dating her, he did, indeed, marry her—though I never heard whether or not he ever collected his winnings from that wager.

Wallace was always beloved by children in his neighborhood. Before he had to retire, he used to drive an old ice cream truck. On Saturdays he would clean all the ice out of the truck and have snowball fights with the kids.

Wally loved to laugh, even if the target of the laughter was himself. There was the time after he and his wife got new carpet in their house and the front door was dragging against the carpet. Wally took the door down off its hinges, sawed off the bottom of the door, and put it back up. Since it still dragged, he took it down again and sawed more off. When he put it back up, it still dragged the floor. That is when he glanced up and realized he had cut several inches off the top of the door.

Then there was the time he missed church and his wife, Thelma, couldn't tell me what was wrong with him without laughing.

"He will have to tell you," she said.

When I ran by to see him, I discovered he had a broken toe.

He explained, "I went out to my garden barr-footed and I noticed something had been eating my termaters. Then I saw this little toadie frog, and I said, 'Little toadie frog, you done been eatin' my termaters. I'm gonna kick you out of my garden.' And when I kicked, I hit this iron post that was sticking up out of the ground."

If you are lucky in this life, you occasionally run into someone like Wallace Brock who overflowed with kindness.

Thomas Evatt

I was blessed to have the Rev. Tom Evatt as the pastor emeritus of Francis Asbury UMC when I arrived. Tom had led that church in its heyday—its very early days in the 1950s when the church was exploding with new members. Now he had returned to Greenville because of a serious heart condition that had forced his early retirement.

But in spite of his health concerns, he was my right-hand man and then some. Because of his long association with the church and its members, he was often the first one called in times of death or hospitalizations, and this gave me more free time than the other places I had worked. With a toddler and a kindergartner plus elderly parents nearby, I needed that time.

Tom seemed to have an endless supply of joy and energy in spite of his grave illness. It is hard for me to picture him when he wasn't laughing and telling a funny story. Often he was laughing so hard at the joke he barely could finish it. He also was a man of deep compassion and zeal for Christ, and these attributes endeared him to our church and to me. And Tom didn't mind grabbing a tiger by the tail when it became necessary, as it did one time at another church in the Midlands right before he became disabled.

In that church there was a troubled man who worked at the local textile mill. The man's alcoholism got the better of him, and Tom convinced the man to seek help by going to a rehabilitation center. But before the man could enter the treatment program, he was fired by his supervisor—also a member of Tom's church. So Tom went over the supervisor's head all the way up to the big boss of the mill and got the man reinstated in his job provided he successfully completed the alcohol rehabilitation program.

When the supervisor heard what Tom had done, he was furious.

"Why didn't you come to talk with me first? Why did you go to the Big Boss with your concern?"

Tom replied, "Because I knew you weren't going to do one damn thing to help your employee."

You didn't mess with Tom unless you wanted to know how he really felt.

I would ask Tom to preach for me several times a year. For one thing, the congregation loved for him to speak. For another thing, there were a series of sayings Tom found a way to weave into every sermon, and it was a fun game to keep listening for those "Tomisms." There was something very comforting about hearing them. One young man who had grown up in the church devised a game whereby he would write down these sayings in advance and then check them off when they appeared in the sermon.

Tom's optimistic outlook on life was summed up this way in his sermons: "I'm like Mary Martin in South Pacific. I'm stuck like a dope with a thing called hope, and I can't get it out of my heart!"

He would reference a church that was always having problems this way: "That church was born in the afflicative case and it lives in the kickative mood!"

When it was time to emphasize a point he want to make sure you heard, Tom would say, "Let me tell you one thing, my dear brothers and sisters."

And Tom never quite got Philippians 4:7 quite right, but we knew what he meant. His benediction for us was always "May the peace of God, which PATHESS all understanding, keep your heart and minds through Christ Jesus." Elizabethan English is difficult for all of us to speak!

It was my privilege to accept a prestigious award during our Annual Conference one year—not for me, but on behalf of Tom who was not able to attend the conference session because of his health condition. I stood there proudly accepting on Tom's behalf an evangelism award that recognized his consistent work across many years in bringing new people into faith in Christ and membership in the church. He did this in spite of his very serious heart ailment.

Tom and his wonderful wife, Inez, decided to leave Greenville and move to our Methodist home, The Oaks, in Orangeburg when I was finishing up my appointment at Francis Asbury in the early 1990s. When Tom decided on a best course of action, he moved quickly and decisively. It is said people at nursing homes live longer and healthier and with fewer worries than those who stay in their own homes, and this was very true of Tom. Because he never surrendered to his illness, he continued his pastoral ministry even after moving to Orangeburg.

I remember riding with Tom in his golf cart over the bumps and hills as we made pastoral calls to our church members who had also moved to The Oaks. His weak heart never stopped Tom from fulfilling his calling to serve God.

And when at last Tom received his call home to eternity, he was in his late eighties. Well done, faithful servant of God.

The Mount Holly Trinity

I was appointed to Mount Holly United Methodist Church in Rock Hill in 1992 as the new pastor, right after the church had completed the building of a Family Life Center. It probably would never have been built had it not been for the "Old Man," as some folks called Paul Rutherford.

Paul was from Texas, and since everything in Texas is big, it comes as no surprise that Paul was a mountain of a man. He was too large—both tall and broad—to fit into the local hospital's CT scan machine and had to go to Charlotte to find one big enough. He also slumped over a bit when he walked, making him look like he could drag his knuckles if his arms were a few inches longer.

Paul was twice retired, once from Duke Power ("Duke Pire" as he called it) and again from Bowater Paper Mill.

The problem with building the Family Life Center was that the church was landlocked. Local building codes prohibited the building of such a huge structure so close to the right-of-way for Highway 901. But there was a small picnic shelter Paul had helped build a few years earlier, and he and the building committee convinced the county zoning officials that what the church was, in fact, building was a rather large addition to the tiny picnic shelter.

It was either that ploy, or else the zoning board's realization that Paul would never give up, that led them to approve the building.

To help raise money for kitchen equipment, several groups took turns preparing a meal for the church on Wednesday nights. Paul, along with his committee and especially his partners in crime Maxine Lacey and Quinton Rogers, prepared the meal several times each month. Those three people and I had lots of laughs together as we quickly bonded and enjoyed kidding one another. I referred to Maxine as "Lacy Drawers" although they called her "Whirlwind" because of how fast she darted from place to place. They all were good at pranks, but I especially had to keep alert for Paul's wit.

At a supper one Wednesday evening, I was a few minutes late. I hurried to a microphone to say a blessing.

"We've already had a blessing," I was told.

I wanted to know who had said the prayer and someone pointed to Paul.

"Paul? When did Paul learn how to pray?" I quipped.

He lowered his fork to his plate as he replied, "Last June, right after you got here."

Paul loved to tell people that, a few months before I was appointed to Mount Holly, he had called the bishop to advise him about the type of pastor the church needed. A few months after I arrived, he called the bishop once again to complain because the bishop had apparently ignored his advice.

The bishop replied, "I did exactly what you asked me, Paul. You said for me to appoint the best pastor I had or nothing at all, and Arthur is the nearest to nothing I have!"

There was a ball field right next to the parsonage, and early one morning, lightning struck the ball field's metal fence. That blast of energy knocked out the well pumps of four or five houses near the ball field, and it also got my TVs and my computer. Destroyed along with the computer were the copies of all my sermons, prompting Paul to say, "Well, now! Never mind what we might think of your sermons. You just heard from the Almighty."

Quinton was another story. He once poured a gallon of gasoline into a coworker's car every day for a week, causing the man to think he was getting phenomenal mileage from his new Volkswagen Beetle. Then the next week, Quinton syphoned some gasoline out of the man's car every day, causing the man to take his VW to the dealer for repairs.

One time, Quinton came by the church on a Friday and asked where I was. Our secretary said, "He is off today." Then Quinton asked her, "How can you tell?"

Maxine led a weekly Bible study for older folks, and she was the van driver whenever the Young at Heart club went on an outing. Together with Paul and Quinton, Maxine was always willing to cook a meal, whether for a youth mission team of fifty youth, or for our Rock Hill District pastors, or for any other group. It was at one of those preachers' meetings that they gave me one of my most prized treasures. Earlier they had dressed me up in a cowboy slicker as part of our "Pony Express" stewardship program. Now they were publicly presenting me with a picture of me in that cowboy outfit. But it was the picture frame that stood out. It was an old toilet seat, the kind that has an opening at the front, making it look like a very large horseshoe. My ministerial colleagues were duly impressed.

I never had a problem these guys wouldn't try to fix. Once Penny backed into a tree in the parking lot of a music store, and it put quite a dent in the rear bumper. While I was visiting someone at the hospital, Paul and Quinton took the bumper off her car, removed the plastic cover, and placed the bumper on a stack of blocks, making the bumper a ramp from the ground up to the top of the stack of blocks. Then Paul drove his truck up that ramp, thereby straightening out the bumper. When I got back, they were putting the bumper back on the car. Some people seem to know how to fix anything.

The history of the church needed updating, and Paul undertook this task. I often kidded him about his hunt-and-peck typing with his oversized, crooked fingers. He talked the church into buying a scanner so pictures and old records could be saved digitally for the future. With Paul's help, we learned Mount Holly UMC was founded in the 1840s as Shiloh Church by a group of Presbyterians from the Fishing Creek Presbyterian Church near Chester, South Carolina. The deed to the church stated the building could be used by all denominations in order to prevent collusion—perhaps collusion that eventually led to the Civil War. After the war, the Presbyterians moved further out in the country, leaving the Methodists to use the old church building. But for some reason, that original building was abandoned, as was the name Shiloh, and the Methodists crossed the road to build Mount Holly Methodist Church, South. The old church building became a barn or a stable for horses that children rode to Mount Holly School, which was built next to the old abandoned church. Someone said the fact that the old church had become a horse stable was the reason the bishop continued appointing "donkeys" to Mount Holly, and they looked right at me when they said that!

I had a fairly good idea why the old church had been abandoned and the congregation had relocated. I figured the Methodists could not get a clear title to the old church, and without that title the annual conference would never agree to a new building going up on that site. Paul continued pushing and pushing for an answer. Finally, a granddaughter of a "presiding elder" from the 1870s found an old book of quarterly conference minutes, and in those minutes we found the substantiation for my theory.

Mount Holly United Methodist Church was never on my list of churches I had hoped to be appointed to. Our family wanted to stay in Greenville, where we were happy and where we were very close to my recently widowed mother. I was actually told by my district superintendent that I would be staying in Greenville, but at the last minute some appointments had to be shuffled and my name landed beside "Mount Holly" on the bishop's list of appointments. We pastors took an oath to go wherever we are appointed, without reservation, and so we packed our belongings and our sad children and moved to Rock Hill.

I think back to how depressed I was at moving and now marvel at how fortunate we were. I almost missed out on knowing all those good folks at Mount Holly. I would have missed getting pinched on my leg by Mrs. Callie White when I told her

I was going to dress up like her for Halloween because she was so scary!

"You go home and explain to your wife how you got that blue mark on your leg at Bible Study," Mrs. Callie quipped.

I would have missed playing one last season on a church softball team and watching my two children learning to play sports at church. The two "best men" at our son's wedding were friends from that community, and the three of them still get together every year for a mini-vacation trip.

Most of all, I would never have known Maxine, Quinton, and Paul, who never seemed to run out of time to give to their church and its pastor.

Thank you, bishop, for messing up my appointment!

Gene and Margaret Simpson

If the truth be known, as they say, many of the people who have joined the United Methodist Church of the Covenant across the years did so because of Gene and Margaret Simpson. First of all, they cannot do enough for the church and its members. If there is any need, they are there "with boots on the ground." If you visit the church, you will be invited out to Sunday lunch with their group of friends.

But what keeps you coming back is Margaret's sweetness and Gene's craziness.

When we moved into the church parsonage on a Wednesday afternoon in June 1998, we met Gene and Margaret, our backyard neighbors. They were very helpful, but I was somewhat unprepared for the reaction I received from a comment I made on my first Sunday. All I said was, "I have already met one of your church's leaders, Gene Simpson," and laughter broke out all over the sanctuary. I knew I was in for an interesting treat having Gene as a church member and a neighbor.

Gene—or Carlton, as he was named originally—was raised by his Simpson grandparents. He was a graduate of Candler School of Theology at Emory University and spent a few years appointed to United Methodist churches in North Carolina. Then Gene moved on into the field of education as dean of students at the newly organized Spartanburg Technical College (now Spartanburg Community College) before landing a job in the Spartanburg industrial community.

Wherever Gene worked or worshiped, he was the perpetrator and the recipient of many practical jokes. Along the way, he developed the reputation of being a tightwad penny-pincher, and to some degree he earned this reputation.

For instance, there was that time Gene hopped over the fence to "offer" me the use of a rented limb shredder in an hour or so, after he finished using it. "Oh, by the way, have you got any gas?" I did, and so Gene filled the shredder's tank. I went with him to see how this gizmo worked, which it sort of did if you first broke the large sticks up into smaller ones. After watching us stumbling and mumbling, Margaret came outside, revved up the lawnmower, and ran over the remaining sticks with her mower, chopping them up into fine mulch and finishing our job. As I moved the shredder over to my side of the fence, Gene mentioned the cost of the rented shredder was forty dollars if I wanted to pay half, which I gladly did. When I returned the shredder to Gene later in the day, I learned he was returning it to the official renter, Bill Funderburk, a church member and a neighbor who lived across the street from Gene, who had paid the other half of the rental. So Gene used my gas, Bill's twenty dollars, my twenty dollars, and got free use of the shredder. That's Gene!

Another time I returned home to find my garden hose turned on and stretched out into Gene's yard. Of course, there was a good reason. A small fire was burning in the corner of his yard, and since his garden hose was not long enough, he used mine to douse the fire. But this was too good an opportunity for me to pass up, and when I had finished my retelling of the story, I had embellished it so Gene was accused of frequently watering his lawn and flowers with water from my house. On other occasions, I implied Gene connected my hose to his waterline so he could supply his house with water from my meter. Church members loved to hear my stories about Gene—and they believed some of them.

Then there was the time we were eating breakfast at Waffle House, sitting at the table next to two zany ladies from the church. Gene's craziness is contagious. One of the women said, "It looks like gentlemen would offer to pay the bill of ladies they know."

I replied, "Too bad there aren't two gentlemen sitting here..."

And Gene added, "Or two ladies sitting there."

I moved to another church appointment in 2004 and then retired in 2012. There were many reasons we bought a house near the Church of the Covenant and returned there to be a part of the church, but Gene and Margaret were two of the biggest reasons we did so.

Perry

Another colorful person I met on my journey around the South Carolina Annual Conference was Perry Thomas. Perry was a retired special agent with the National Security Agency, advising presidents from Ike to Reagan. After Gary Powers' plane was shot down over Russia, Perry advised Ike to come clean about the incident. "They will have the plane as proof, Mr. President." But Eisenhower was a former general who didn't take advice well from a chief master sergeant. I guess he preferred having egg on his face, because Perry was right.

When I was appointed to the Church of the Covenant, I heard a lot about Perry, but I had to wait for three months for him to return from an RV tour of Alaska before I met this character.

Some of the stories told about Perry sounded like he came from a bygone era in the American Wild West. After four days of dating his future bride, Shelby, he proposed to her and she accepted. But she was afraid to tell her father, who could be hard to deal with, especially if he'd had a few too many drinks. Perry told her not to be afraid, that he would handle her father. So they drove out to Shelby's home, where Perry asked his future father-in-law to come over to his car.

Reaching inside his glove compartment, he produced a pistol. Pointing up at two pinecones at the top of a tall pine tree, Perry invited his future father-in-law to watch carefully as he fired off two shots, causing both pinecones to fall to the ground.

Then Perry put the gun away in his glove compartment and announced, "I'm going to marry your daughter. Any questions?"

I am sure military life will never be the same, thanks to Perry. An air raid near his Vietnam base caused everybody to stop what they were doing and head into shelters. For some USO girls, it meant leaving their performance on the stage. But for Perry, it meant leaving the shower, all lathered up and unrinsed. Because of his lather and his lack of clothing, Perry went into one of the darkest corners of the shelter where he thought he was hidden from sight—until he heard one of the USO girls say,

"Come over here, girls, look at what I found."

Nobody liked a laugh at himself more than Perry.

Perry could be a provocative member of the church, usually provoking in a way I approved of. His faith was simple: "Jesus loves me, this I know." About everything else was debatable. He had little tolerance for biblical literalism, saying that many things in the Bible were additions to God's laws put there by man.

I never will forget the heads that turned when Perry asked his Sunday school class, "Do you think that God would condemn a crazy person to hell?" When folks said that a just God would not condemn an insane person, Perry said, "Well, then, you'd better get used to the idea of seeing Hitler in heaven because that man was crazy!"

At Perry's funeral—and this went against everything in our worship committee guidelines—as we were leaving the service, his wife played the recording of "North to Alaska" as our postlude.

Somehow it was very fitting.

Ann Mayfield

Every Christmas Eve candle-lighting communion worship service is inspiring and memorable, but probably none were as memorable and un-inspirational as the one we had at Memorial United Methodist Church in Greer back in 2008 or 2009. The sanctuary was decorated as usual—Chrismon Tree, candles in windows, wreathes on all the doors, and garland suspended down from the balcony. The sanctuary was nearing maximum capacity because out-of-town guests were also there with their Greer families. It was going to be just like the one the previous year, we thought. There is something comforting about the sameness of this annual worship service.

As the choir began singing their anthem, I heard a buzz of conversation all over the sanctuary. How rude, I thought. Then I noticed that everybody was looking away from the choir up toward the corner of our very high ceiling, and just as I turned to look for myself, the object of everyone's attention took flight. Its erratic trajectory indicated that it was a bat and not a bird! After one lap around the sanctuary, he finally returned to his "perch."

I looked back at our church organist, Ann Mayfield. Ann is a tiny little lady. I think she needs a booster seat to reach the organ manuals and platform shoes to reach the pedals. She is also somewhat excitable, and that's why I had to check out her reaction to our "guest."

Her facial expression said it all. She was not looking at the choir director or the printed music—she was playing from memory as she kept her eyes on that bat at all times.

Somehow we all made it through that service. I did notice many people received communion that evening with heads bowed and one eye looking up at the ceiling. I showed I was clearly rattled when I invited everyone to join in the closing prayer, which was printed on "Highway 11." Ann remained at her station until the end, even though I fully expected her to sneak out a back door from the choir loft unnoticed.

In the months following that service, I couldn't help myself. I kept kidding Ann about our visitor. One morning when she was practicing, I took a small paperback devotional booklet and flung it into the choir loft in the direction of the organ. As I hoped it would, it looked and sounded like a bird flapping its wings. Ann took the rear exit in a hurry. Then I found a plastic bat left over from Halloween decorations and suspended it over the organ.

I knew I would face retribution someday, but I wasn't prepared for how she got even.

Several months went by, and one day she and our choir director invited me for breakfast at my favorite restaurant, Waffle House. When the day came, Ann called to say the choir director was out of town but she still wanted to buy my breakfast. As a daily "regular" at the Waffle House, I was used to pranks and jokes being played on me and other regulars, and even the waitresses and cooks.

But I was caught off guard at the sight of Ann, coming from the back of the store … to serve me a "roadkill" breakfast of a toy stuffed squirrel on Texas toast!

Mary Hayes

I arrived in Greer in June 2004 and was told the very first visit I had to make was to Mary Hayes because she embodied all the good things about Memorial United Methodist Church. I did, and they were right. Like so many others in the church, Mary had spent her pre-retirement years in public education, serving for many years as a counselor at Greer High School. She was dearly loved by all her former students, and she kept up with so many of them.

Mary was still able to live at home at that time, but she was very hard of hearing and almost blind, even with the help of hearing aids and glasses. Visits with her were not easy, but they were very enjoyable. She taught Sunday school at least once a month and attended worship every Sunday. She was able to follow the worship service fairly well because of the amplification system in the sanctuary, plus we gave her (and others with hearing difficulties) a large printed copy of the sermon every week. This meant I had to have my sermon finalized and ready to be printed by noon on Friday, and this externally applied discipline made me a much-better prepared preacher than I had previously been.

Mary had such a joy about her, and she loved to laugh. One time when she had missed church, we mailed her the printed sermon, which someone then read to her. She later told me, "I enjoyed your sermon. It was very good! I was wondering ... who wrote it for you?"

Like many schoolteachers, especially those of her era, Mary had a strong sense of right and wrong. But nothing was ever beyond grace and love for her former students, even if they went astray. When a young unmarried woman became pregnant, there were many of the usual reactions in our church and community, and Mary heard some of the gossip. So she called me to come to her house. She wanted to know what I and the church were doing to offer our love and support to that young woman and her family, and I was pleased to tell her we were having a baby shower and that her friends were standing right there beside her with their love and support.

She responded by saying, "Good. They'd better!"

Mary carried so much weight that her word alone would have quieted all criticisms in that community.

Eventually Mary became unable to see or hear well enough to stay at her home, and so she moved to the new nursing home cottages in Greer. I didn't feel like I could speak as loudly in her room there as I had at her own home, and that made our visits more difficult. But she continued having the sermons read to her, and she enjoyed the visits from her church friends and also her former colleagues at Greer High. She outlasted me as her pastor, and I had to slip back over to see her after I retired, with or without the approval of my pastoral successor.

Ms. Mary died at the blessed old age of ninety-six, three years after I moved away from Greer.

Bill Crotzer

Each of us has an index in our brains, actually several of them, like a computer database. When we need to identify a color, our index scrolls through our brain's color index until we find a match.

My wife knew a college music professor once who had perfect pitch, and whenever he heard a car horn or a train whistle, he would stop his class lecture and call out the pitch he just heard. His musical pitch index was the dominant one in his life. Others know all the Shakespearean plays and know where every quote comes from.

I have two such dominant indexes, and one is the songs of the 1960s. If I hear a few bars, I can usually name that tune. The other index is jokes. Often a song or a joke comes to mind as a response to someone's Facebook posts. It's natural to me.

I haven't met many people with a joke index like mine, but I met one back in 2018 when I was interim pastor at Gaffney's Buford Street United Methodist Church. Retired banker Bill Crotzer was eighty-nine when we met. His first comment to me was a joke, and it set off my index and so I fired one right back at him. This went on for about five or ten minutes until one of us surrendered!

The other people who had gathered around us had long since walked away. But we knew we would become friends, and we did. Bill did have one talent I'll never be accused of having—he was quite the artist.

But there was something else I will always remember about my friend Bill. Christianity was woven into the fabric of his life and soul. He didn't try to be Christian. Christianity was always present within him, looking for an opportunity to come out of his soul onto whoever needed his word of grace. That was true almost fifty years ago after his own teenaged son was struck and killed while trick-or-treating. Not many men would have gone by to visit the young driver who had just caused his son's death, but Bill did. He told the young driver he knew his son's death had been caused by an accident and that the teen would need to learn to live with his mistake, and he forgave the boy right then and there. Bill had a Christlike index that was bigger than his joke index.

My friend Bill died at home in December 2021 at age ninety-two. I know that just as soon as Bill was escorted through the pearly gates, he had a joke or two ready to tell St. Peter. Knowing Bill, that conversation might still be going on.

Mentors

I laugh every time I see someone who claims to be a self-made man (or woman). To be self-made, you would have to crawl out of your crib and change your own diaper!

I readily admit I stand on my mom and dad's shoulders. I had a head start in life some folk don't have.

I also had a head start in spiritual formation. My church, my family, my teachers (in school and church), and my pastors all gave me a "leg up" when it came to my life's work as a pastor. In fact, if I am due any credit, it is that I realized at age twenty-five that unless I got trained by a good pastor and a good seminary that I would never have any chance to be successful and useful to God.

The next section of this book contains stories about some of those wonderful mentors. I am way too young to have ever personally walked with Jesus, but these mentors were taught by generations of disciples of those who did walk with Jesus many years ago, and I was so blessed to learn more about my Lord from these individuals.

The Rev. Dr. Ed Ellis

Ed Ellis was appointed as the associate pastor of my home church, Bethel United Methodist Church, in June 1968, a few weeks after I completed high school and a few months before I started Wofford College. Part of his responsibilities was leading our youth ministry, and he arrived in time to tackle a huge division in our youth group.

The reason for the strife, that I was a huge part of, was that many members of our eighty-member youth group had recently experienced a renewal of their faith during a weekend retreat and others of us had not. In fact, my faction couldn't understand why the members of the other side had felt the need for their faith renewal experience. We had grown up together from the nursery to the present. All of us had previously professed faith in Christ, and some of us thought this was a case of emotionalism and fanaticism. The other side reacted to our doubts about them as doubts about God. They figured we must not be Christians—that we also needed a renewal "experience" before we could understand them.

Lucky for me, I left home for the summer to be a counselor at our Methodist camp up in the South Carolina mountains.

It really bothered my side that our religious experience was not considered adequate. It bothered the other side that their experience was not taken seriously, that it was considered to be shallow emotionalism.

It would take a person of great perception and wisdom to reunite our splintered youth group, and Ed accomplished this within three months of his arrival.

Ed's own faith story had much more in common with my opponents. In fact, he always enjoyed calling me "Saul of Tarsus, persecutor of the Christians." Ed had come into faith through a conversion experience as a young adult. But his seminary training had given him another insight.

He told our group that there were two ways to smooth a rough rock. The rock could be put in a rock tumbler and smoothed quickly overnight, like those who had recently had a faith awakening, or else the rock could be placed in a river where the current would reshape the rock over many years, like some of us who had been shaped by God over a lifetime of spiritual formation through Christian education. With that simple illustration, he enabled the two factions of our youth group to acknowledge the validity of each other's faith experience, and peace returned to the valley.

His guidance freed me from my fear of emotionalism and even freed me to have my own deepening religious experiences over the next few years. One of the things I have been able to do throughout my ministry has been to affirm a person's faith experience, even if it falls far outside the norm. Rejected people shut down emotionally and spiritually. Loved and accepted people keep growing.

It is hard for me to imagine Ed as a long-haired, bleached-blond teenager, but that is what he was as a teenager. He was raised by his mother; his father gave him his name but not much else.

Ed was not a good student or a happy person during high school. He wrote about his life in the July-August 1996 issue of the Upper Room devotional booklet: "I had an English teacher who was adored by the student body. One day in class he asked each student to share their plans after graduation. Most named the college they planned to attend. Desperately wanting to be among the elite group, I named a college. The teacher responded in a sarcastic voice, 'You aren't going to any college. You are not college material.'" Ed described the "consuming hate" that he developed for this teacher.

But after a classmate led him to Christ the next year, that hate mellowed into determination. Before Ed closed his book satchel, he had degrees from Spartanburg Methodist (Junior) College and St. Andrews University, his Master of Theology from Duke University, and his Doctorate in Ministries from McCormick Theological Seminary in Chicago. He also had a drive to advance in his career in ministry, and he managed to be appointed to some of our biggest United Methodist churches.

So the sarcasm of that teacher led to a highly successful life, educationally and vocationally, for Ed.

When Ed was at Bethel, his senior pastor was Dr. Francis Cunningham. Ed enjoyed saying this about their partnership: "He is St. Francis and I am his Assisi." I was happy to ask the Assisi to place his hand on my head, along with the bishop's hand and Julian Lazar's hand, as I was ordained elder in The United Methodist Church.

There were several other times later in my life when our paths crossed. One time was right after my best friend from college died suddenly at age thirty-three from a brain aneurism. I was devastated. I really had not lost anyone close to me since my grandfather died twenty-two years earlier, and my faith suffered a direct hit. How can things like this happen when God is Lord of the universe, I wondered.

I turned to Ed for his wise counsel. Ed's explanation was that when God was creating the world God could have chosen perfect orderliness with no illness, no pain, no death—but to do so would have meant that humans would have to be puppets without real freedom of choice. Absence of free choice is a meaningless existence, and God opted for meaning over orderliness. For love to have any meaning, there had to be the possibility of loss of love. For life to be considered precious, death had to be a possibility. In a very real way, the all-powerful God chose to limit God's-self so humans could be free and experience meaning.

That helped me hang onto God at that difficult time in my life until I could further process my growing theology.

Twenty years later, I started going by Ed's house frequently because he was caring for his daughter, Lorraine, during her final illness. Cancer had already taken his wife, Iris, from him, and now it was taking his only child. He was amazing in the care and comfort he gave her, and I and others paid him visits to give him encouragement.

It is a great testimony to his values that after his wife and daughter died, Ed gave a huge donation to the school that started him in his educational journey, Spartanburg Methodist College. The school responded by naming the first environmentally "green" educational building in South Carolina "Ellis Hall" in his honor. By then he was happily remarried to Dr. Charlotte Lindler Ellis, a retired pediatrician with Pediatric Associates in Columbia.

Ed came along at precisely the right time to get me started off in my adult life, advising me on many matters and also performing our wedding ceremony. I was twenty-one when the love bug bit and Penny and I decided to get married even before I finished college. Not saying that I was nervous, but Ed later told me that when he saw me standing there with my pale white face, he prayed, "Lord, don't let Arthur faint!"

The Rev. Adger McKay

One of my pastoral mentors was a remarkable man named Adger McKay. When I met him in 1968, he was leading a Thursday night home Bible study, traveling each week to Spartanburg, South Carolina, from Montreat, North Carolina. Love offerings from these Bible studies and from speaking engagements were Adger's main means of income, but he and his brother also farmed together. Never in all my life have I known anyone remotely like Adger. He absolutely exuded faith, joy, peace, and love. Nor have I known anyone whose heart seemed to belong to God so completely as did his.

Adger was home in North Carolina after being a Presbyterian missionary in Mexico for some years. From what I could piece together about his missionary life, he had grown discouraged with the lack of fruits of his labor and had almost stopped all unnecessary activities. He concentrated his efforts on a small number of pastors and laypeople, and together they spent hours in prayer for revival. Finally revival did happen, and he was busier than ever. But in the process, he had become a charismatic Presbyterian, and although he never said it, it is my impression that this change closed the doors for Adger to continue as a missionary.

Back in Montreat, Adger and his wife, Ann, and their children continued attending their Presbyterian Church (the same one Billy Graham belonged to), and I never heard him say one bad thing about his denomination. In fact, he is probably the one person responsible for keeping my feet in the church during those days of the late 1960s and early 1970s when the Vietnam War caused a lot of us college kids to distrust all institutions.

"If you leave your church," he would admonish us, "who will take the life of Christ that you have experienced to the members of the church?" He would also say, "Over the years, the historic church has stood for God in this world, and so we cannot just abandon it."

He didn't see much hope in the new churches that were springing up from the revival era in which we lived then. "In twenty-five years, that church will be just like the one those folks are leaving right now, so stay where you are," he would warn us.

Adger was a spellbinding speaker. His faith was so alive, and the life of Christ flowed out of him. He would have considered himself an exhorter—an encourager—rather than an evangelist or pastor. He would read an entire passage of Scripture and then go back to the first verse, bringing it and subsequent verses to life by using illustrations from his own life. He was often encouraged to form an association like other evangelists, but he shunned all such suggestions.

"Too many people are busy building their own kingdoms rather than the kingdom of God," was his answer. "Besides, if God opens the door a crack, I'll be back in Mexico."

Adger was always there when I needed him, encouraging me in my faith journey. He kept my feet on the ground, and he kept me from chasing the latest religious fad. "God is doing more than that, Arthur," he'd say, reminding me to keep my focus on the big picture.

It was through Adger that a call to ministry for me was confirmed. One week after we met, he said to me, "God is calling you to ministry in his church to teach the ways of Jesus." Then he quickly added, "Now don't you go and fulfill that word—wait and see if, indeed, God fulfills it."

Sometimes while I was in college, I would drive up to Montreat to see him when I was really discouraged. The phone would ring, interrupting our visit, and someone would begin pouring out their heart to Adger, confessing to some shortcoming.

"You know, God will forgive you for that," I would hear him say.

Adger died in about 1978 after having contracted a rare form of malaria while on a missionary journey. His wife, Ann, said this about her husband's death: "Adger walked so closely with God that I doubt he even noticed the transition between this life and heaven."

Adger had some favorite sayings that I remember so well because they are still part of me today. I may not have the words verbatim, but I have captured the essence as I remember these "Adgerisms."

"The letter kills but the Spirit gives life. If you spend all your time reading the Scriptures, you will dry up. If you never read the Word and rely totally upon the Spirit (fellowship and prayer), you'll blow up. But if you balance Bible reading with the Spirit, you'll grow up."

"Brethren ... and sistren ..."

"So many people have this picture of God: He is looking down from heaven, watching for people to mess up so that he can punish them. No, friends. That is not the God we worship. God is looking down from heaven, looking over your lives, looking for reasons and opportunities to bless you, not curse you."

"God is a big God. He will even bless our best efforts for him, bless our attempts to serve him, even if ministries are born of flesh and not God's Spirit. That is how big God is. But he would rather that we wait upon him to see what he would have us do, and when we are acting on the Spirit's leading, his blessing will really abide in the work."

"We are hung up on huge numbers. But God would rather have five people in this town whose hearts belong to God, who have sold out to him, than hundreds of half-committed disciples. With only five committed followers, God can turn this city upside down."

"Predestination and free will seem to be two lines that will never meet—never cross. But I am sure that in God's eternity they do. Both must be true. Moody had a dream about this. He was standing outside the gates of heaven where there was a sign that said, 'Whosoever will.' He decided to walk inside the gate, and once inside, he looked back up at the sign and from the inside the sign said, 'Foreordained since the foundation of the earth.'"

Sometimes I would ask him about the end times. "The Jews are back in control of Jerusalem like they have to be before Christ returns," I would say.

"Yes, but they could lose it again," he'd say. "This might not be 'the' time."

And when I asked him about what I have come to know is Darby's scheme of the end-time (Anti-Christ, Tribulation, Rapture, Second Coming), Adger expressed some questions about this, saying, "If a Tribulation is coming and Christians have the answer, why would God want to take us off the planet? I think some people want the Rapture for the same reason that they want to go to Florida in winter."

His open questioning probably saved me from becoming a follower of Darby.

Philippians 2:13 says, "For it is God who is at work in you, enabling you both to will and to work for his good pleasure."

Adger would say, "People used to tell me to pull myself up by my own bootstraps. That never worked for me. But when I learned that God was at work in me, causing me to will and do his good pleasure, that meant God would stand me up. That is what the Christian faith is to me—God working in me, causing me to will and do his good pleasure."

I have reflected on the following words of Adger many times in recent days. When it came to the change in women's roles in society and when it came to divorce, Adger managed to stay away from harsh attitudes while reminding us of God's ideals.

"You can do that if you choose to," he would tell us. "A lot of people are. We are not under law but under grace, and there is no condemnation to those in Christ Jesus. God will bless you no matter what—that is just how big he is! But if you want God's highest blessing, then you need to follow the teachings of the word."

There was always a load of grace in Adger's life and his words.

Dr. John Benjamin Bedenbaugh

If you happened to see Dr. John Benjamin Bedenbaugh walking across the campus of the Lutheran Theological Southern Seminary in Columbia, South Carolina, during the 1970s, the first thing you would notice about him was his attire. He looked like he had been dressed by a K-Mart "Blue Light Special" agent.

His shoes were the steel-toed variety. His buttoned-down shirt was worn over some bright yellow or blue T-shirt, usually with some writing or logo on it that could be seen shining through his outer shirt like a neon sign. His hair looked like he had made one minor attempt to comb it before he came to class, but his front locks usually flopped over his forehead, causing him to push it back constantly as he lectured.

He looked like a caricature of the absent-minded professor.

One day some prospective students and their parents were present in class when Dr. Bedenbaugh arrived. I don't think he even noticed them. He was already into his lecture when one of them took his picture with a flash camera, making him aware of their presence, and so he stopped to ask them who they were.

One of my Methodist buddies couldn't resist the chance to kid him about his wardrobe: "Actually, Dr. Bedenbaugh, they are with People Magazine and they are here to take the pictures of the 10 best-dressed men on campus."

Never to be beaten in such times of kidding, Dr. Bedenbaugh answered, "We Lutherans are so conscious of being robed in the righteousness of Christ that we don't worry about our outward appearance like you Methodists do."

Not only was his appearance untidy, you should have seen his office and his house. Several years' worth of newspapers were stacked up in a number of piles in both locations. From time to time he would remind us that "creative minds are seldom tidy."

This was the professor we called "Benny"—behind his back, of course—and he became one of the greatest influences on my life and my faith development.

Benny was one of those professors you either liked or disliked. I and many other seminarians initially approached theology as if it were a science or a set of mathematical formulas to be memorized and mastered. If that remained your approach to theology, then Benny would seem to be a very poor theologian. But those of us he so richly blessed were able to change our way of understanding theology to be more like his.

"Theology is not like going to a park with your Kodak and taking a photo of the park because there is no interpretation in a picture like that," he would tell us. "It is more like going to that same park with a canvas and some paint. Your painting won't be an exact reproduction. It will be, rather, an interpretation of that park, interpreted by the painter."

Then he added, "Theology has much more in common with art, music, and literature than it does math and science. It is full of interpretation."

If I had never heard him say another word, that would have been enough to liberate me.

If a student had a fundamentalist or literal view of the Bible, he would not have been comfortable with Benny's approach to the Bible at all. In my case, he freed me from whatever slight vestiges of fundamentalism that were still inside of me.

"Some people would prefer it if the Bible had been lowered on a string from heaven, dictated directly by God, more like the claims about the Book of Mormon," he said. "But a God who would have to dictate his written word or send it directly from heaven would not be Lord of the universe. He would be a very weak God. Only a God who was Lord of the universe would dare to send his incarnate word to earth as he did, risking natural birth to peasant parents who were citizens of a powerless nation. Only a God who was all-powerful would dare to let his only son become a child, risking childhood illnesses. That same God chose to send his written word to us the same way, incarnate in humans. God allowed mortals to experience his word and write it down, using their own native languages. Then God allowed other mortals, sitting in councils, to decide which writings to include in the canon and which ones to exclude."

Benny would remind us that we are not to read the Bible like a law student reads a law book, looking for verses to cite to back up our positions. Rather we are to immerse ourselves in reading the Bible, Benny said, so we become sensitive to the will of God.

I remember one time when a TV advertisement had made the sensational claim that the writings in the Apocrypha and the pseudepigrapha had been suppressed by the church for centuries. One of my church members was very upset by this claim, so I asked Benny what I should tell him.

Benny replied, "Tell him that he doesn't read the sixty-six books he's got now. So why in the hell does he want more?"

Benny also loved to use media in classroom settings. Each January he would take a group of students to his house for his interim class on "The Message in the Media." We would look at shows like "All in the Family" to see how God and the church were portrayed in movies and television shows. It wasn't as much a critique of the media as it was his way of encouraging us to use what everybody was already watching in our sermons and in Christian education settings.

I will always remember the time he showed an old silent movie, "From Soup to Nuts," starring Laurel and Hardy, while playing a soundtrack—I think it was the soundtrack to Bernstein's Mass. It was hilarious and entertaining! Then he gave a ten-minute lecture on the doctrinal themes conjured up by that movie—original sin, legalisms, and biblical literalism.

When I was inspired by some drama students to try my hand at a first-person sermon, Benny insisted I come into class one day dressed as Saul of Tarsus, interrupt his class and tell of "my" Damascus Road conversion. Then he surprised me by saying, "Paul will now hold a press conference to answer any questions you might have." I couldn't believe he had set me up without warning! I was asked about Paul's attitude toward women, and someone wanted to know what Paul's thorn in the flesh was. I decided to BS my way out of that second question by saying, "When I wrote those words, I purposely chose to be vague so that you might see that God can use your weakness, whatever your thorn in the flesh might be."

Benny liked my performance so much that we went on the road together to several Lutheran churches in Columbia.

It seemed we were back on the road doing our two-man act again when the graduates of Lutheran Theological Southern Seminary got together for supper during Annual Conference. Benny was asked to be our guest speaker. He returned to his theme of how theology was so closely connected to art, literature, and music. "Sometimes when I listen to classical music, I get the feeling that Beethoven is making love to me on the piano." Then seeing me in the audience, and knowing that my wife was an accomplished musician, Benny asked, "Arthur, does Penny ever make love to you on the piano?"

There was something about being in Benny's presence that always made my brain quick to react, and so I answered, "No. Our piano is an upright."

After I moved away from the Columbia area, I lost touch with my old friend, and too soon he died after a lengthy battle with cancer. Once during his illness, I wrote him a get-well letter, and in it I tried to summarize what he had meant to me and my faith development.

Benny, I don't know how many other students you helped, but you were the Lutheran seminary to me!

The Rev. Julian Lazar

Each year at Annual Conference, there is a memorial service to honor pastors or spouses who have died during the previous year. At the service of 2002, I was sitting with the Rev. Julian Lazar, honoring the memory of his wife, Sara.

"Tell me the connection with the Lazars," the bishop asked me.

"I'm an adopted Lazar," I replied. "I am not sure whether it is a blessing or a curse, bishop, but I would not be a United Methodist pastor without Julian's influence."

The bishop looked away as if contemplating an appropriate response, and then joked with me, "Well, I think it is a blessing ..."

In the winter of 1972, I was a few months away from college graduation. Although I had been accepted at several theology schools, seminary would have been very difficult for me at that time. For one thing, Penny and I had been married less than a year, and neither of us felt secure moving out of state to a big city and finding jobs. Also, my theology was very unsettled during this time. Although I was raised as a United Methodist and had worked in several Methodist churches during college, I wasn't sure which denomination I would affiliate with. The sense of "call" that pastors talk about was not very clear to me at that time either.

When I heard that a Methodist pastor in nearby Lyman was planning to hire a full-time youth director, I applied for the job and was hired. That pastor was Julian Lazar.

Three months after I began my new job, Julian moved, being appointed to a church in the Columbia, South Carolina, area. But during those ninety days, we formed a deep friendship that has influenced my life like no other friendship ever has. I admired the way he warmly related to people. I admired his ability to be a real human being, accepting himself with his imperfections. I liked his emphasis on God's grace as shown though Christ.

I especially liked the fact that he could laugh at himself when he made verbal slips—like the time at a wedding when he asked the groom, "Do you take this woman to be your lawfully bedded wife?" The groom seemed quite anxious to say, "I do!"

My time with the Lyman Church after Julian left was not a very happy experience for me. I lacked the proper training to be a successful youth worker, and the pastor who came after Julian was hard for me to get to know because he was quite reserved. I am sure he was also concerned about where his not-quite-Methodist youth director was leading his youth. From time to time I would visit Julian and Sara, and each time Julian would urge me to attend seminary and pursue ordained ministry. But I was not sure yet of my call to ministry.

In August 1974, the same week Nixon left the White House, we left South Carolina to move to Roanoke, Virginia, to a farm owned by Penny's aunt and uncle. I began selling insurance (or rather, I was employed by an insurance agency, which wondered when I was going to ever sell any policies). I thought the door to ministry had forever slammed shut.

But as months went by, I found myself thinking about ministry constantly, wanting to find some way to be employed full-time in the Lord's work—and this time I wanted to be successful. Finally I had a sense of urgent call, but I needed a mentor if I was going to succeed.

Meanwhile in Irmo, Julian's youth director left to return to school. One evening in March 1975, my Roanoke phone rang. It was Julian calling to offer me the job and an opportunity to begin seminary at the Lutheran seminary in Columbia. When I expressed some reservations, Julian replied, "Arthur, I am at home, sick with the flu. I haven't talked with the church yet about hiring you, but the Lord told me to call you." With most people, I have learned to question what the Lord supposedly has told them, but I have learned to pay attention when Julian says it!

While employed at Union United Methodist Church in Irmo, I got to observe how Julian succeeded in ministry. I also watched a well-trained Christian education director as she led youth ministry, and I learned about church administration from the business manager of the church. I began seminary and really enjoyed it. By 1979, I had completed Lutheran Seminary and was the ordained associate pastor of the church. By then Julian had moved again and left me with another capable mentor, Jim Nates, who taught me other skills for ministry. And here I am, in the twenty-first century, still trying to copy my mentors Julian and Jim as I continue in ministry during my retirement.

Perhaps one other perspective on our friendship needs to be told. The Lazars had two sons; both have died. I conducted both funerals at Julian and Sara's request. I also delivered the eulogy for Sara's funeral. Since my parents are both dead, and since Julian is now without children, he has claimed me as his son, and I am thankful to claim him as my father. In many ways, these titles are very appropriate. Fathers often help us discover who we are and the direction in life we are to take.

How rare it is that you meet someone who forever changes the course of your life, whose Christian example is so real that it is contagious. The Scripture says Jesus had that effect on people. He just said, "Come follow me," and people left homes and jobs to be with him.

After meeting one of Jesus' disciples named Julian Lazar, I can understand why.

The Rev. Dr. Jim Nates

Whereas Julian Lazar was instrumental in getting me into the ordained ministry, Jim Nates probably did more than anyone else to shape the kind of pastor I became.

I was quite anxious when I learned Julian was being moved from Irmo to Sumter in the summer of 1977. He was the only pastor I had experienced success with. He and I had established a good working relationship as well as a great friendship. So I went to our district superintendent, Chad Davis, to see if it would be best for me if I moved also and allow the new pastor to choose his or her own associate pastor. Chad could not tell me who was about to be appointed to Irmo, but he said he thought I would really like my new boss.

I finally met him at the Annual Conference session, and I will never forget what he said to me. Here I was, wondering how I would have to change to accommodate my new boss, but Jim said something to me that indicated I wouldn't have to change who I was. We would work things out to where we both could be who we are and conduct our ministries in harmony, he said. What an affirmation that was, and I began to look forward to working with him.

It didn't take us long to hit our stride. It was great to see another style of pastoral leadership so I could have two role models. Whereas Julian is such a charismatic personality that all attention focuses on him when he is in a room, Jim seemed comfortable to slip into a group almost unnoticed. While Jim was not in any way reserved, he was very comfortable allowing others to lead. He really tried to make us co-pastors, and his wife, Carolyn, said he had succeeded. I never forgot who the boss was, but it was great to feel like he trusted me as a partner.

Case in point: A family visited our church one Sunday. It was my job to call on our visitors, and I did so, enjoying my visit with the couple and her elderly mother. A few weeks later, the family wanted to join our church. The elderly mother said that she would be ready—as soon as the pastor came by to visit her. Jim responded, "Our pastor did come by to visit you," and he refused to give in to her demand.

The Staff-Parish Relations Committee tried to get Jim to go visit the lady, but he told them, "If I have to go behind Arthur and visit everybody he visits, then we don't need him—or you don't need me." They had to agree, and we all allowed the lady to join another United Methodist church in the area. But her daughter and son-in-law did join our church, and I heard him tell Jim that he enjoyed one hour of peace away from his mother-in-law every week!

It has been said the deeper that sorrow carves into your being, the more joy you can contain (Gibran). Part of the spiritual depth in Jim Nates had been carved by the death by cancer of his firstborn child. I knew that if this man could still preach about the love of God after tasting such sorrow, I needed to listen.

I observed Jim's every move. Watching him was the best education I ever received. When he was upset about something, he very openly and calmly said so. He didn't go off to sulk, and he never exploded in anger. There was the time when our administrative board was so excited that an English exchange pastor who had been with us several years earlier was going to be visiting South Carolina again. We voted to invite him to preach on a certain day, never checking with our pastor to see if this would be OK with him.

Jim waited until we had finished our work, and then he stood up and said calmly and politely, "I am glad your friend will be coming back for a visit, and I look forward to his preaching. But it would have been common courtesy for you to ask your pastor's permission first before you invited someone to fill his pulpit."

Talk about feeling very small. How rude we had been! But the way Jim had handled the situation, we all learned a valuable lesson, and our respect for him grew. And I saw how I should conduct myself in similar circumstances in the future.

Jim's style of preaching was very different from most people I knew. He said he didn't feel close to the congregation when he was in the pulpit (my favorite place to preach), so he walked out in the open chancel area. He didn't move around very much; he just stood there. His mind was so organized that he could speak extemporaneously with no notes to keep him on message. He preferred to wear a white robe instead of our traditional black one. He said white was more celebratory, and worship should be a celebration. Soon I was wearing white, also. For years I wore the formal black robe in fall and winter and the white one from Easter throughout the summer. The first time I wore white in one congregation, I heard an old man exclaim, "It's Jesus Christ!" Not quite.

One of the things I was proudest of was the fact that we set about to intentionally form a theologically diverse congregation. Our church had a group of charismatics; we had some fundamentalists; there were the lifelong United Methodists and some former Baptists. Some were quite liberal; others were very conservative. Together Jim and I held out the hope that there was a place at our church for all of those people—as long as they remembered to love one another. Jim set the stage for this with a sermon titled, "The Bottom Line and our Brands." The bottom line was Peter's confession: Jesus is the Christ. The various theological positions were our brands. It worked pretty well, though not perfectly. Some folks couldn't buy into this vision, but others of us thrived in it.

I have always had a quick wit, but I had met my match in Jim. Never did I get the better of him. At our midweek church dinners, I would make the announcements and then tell some joke on Jim as he was coming up to deliver a devotional. He was always ready for me, having a better joke to tell on me.

Jim was a marathon runner and he talked about it in many sermons, and so I began calling him "Jogging Jimmy." Since I was usually telling some kind of foolishness and never exercised, he called me "Sitting Bull." I even re-wrote and performed a Ray Stevens song, "I Need Your Help, Barry Manilow." My version was called, "I Need Your Help, Jogging Jimmy Nates," and it had this memorable line, "If you did not jog, what would you preach about?"

We really enjoyed our time together. I will never forget a soloist who performed the song "This is My Task" at our early service. This song has a very high series of notes in the introduction, and those high notes threw our soloist off. He never found his right notes. Verse one was sung in an extremely high falsetto. Verse two was sung in a very low bass. Verse three sounded like Chinese harmony. I didn't dare look at Jim. I knew we would both lose it.

A little boy on the front pew said, "Mommy, what wong wid dat man?" Jim and I both bit our lips and made it through the solo.

Then later, as we were riding home from dinner at our lay leader's home, Jim's daughter Jennifer asked, "Daddy, what was wrong with that man this morning?" The pent up laughter in both of us exploded, and Jim had to park the car on the side of the road so that we could laugh and cry without having a wreck.

I graduated from the Lutheran Theological Southern Seminary in May 1979, cum laude no less. That's not bad for someone who had been afraid of going to seminary, and both Jim and Julian were there to congratulate me. I stayed on with Jim at Irmo until February 1981 (almost four years) when I was moved mid-year to Saluda, South Carolina. I agreed to the appointment, but I sure missed my partner. At least we could get together occasionally for tennis. But I have remarked many times in the various places I had lived and worked, "On my best days, you are seeing my imitation of Jim Nates."

Many years have gone by. As of this writing, I am seventy-two years old and retired. Julian and Jim are both in their nineties now. Both of my mentors have mentioned their desire for me to deliver their funeral eulogies, and I always say "If you don't preach my funeral first!"

I will tell you this: I have never seen Jesus with my own eyes, but he has to be as gracious as my mother, and he has to be as good, kind, and wise as Julian Lazar and Jim Nates.

How I Became a Marginal Preacher

Perhaps this tale from my past can now be safely told! It is the tale of how I became an ordained United Methodist pastor.

Back in the 1970s, The United Methodist Church had two ordinations for pastors. First, candidates for ministry would be ordained "deacon" when they had completed one-fourth of seminary, been a member of a local UMC for a year, and if they had received the endorsement of their local church and home district. Then a few years later, after they finished seminary and served a year or more in a local church, they could be ordained "elder." (That process was changed a few years ago; now candidates are "commissioned" and then later ordained an elder or a deacon depending on whether one is becoming a pastor or a youth or children's worker, or a musician.)

In 1976, I was working in Irmo at Union UMC while attending seminary, but my home district was Spartanburg. My seminary friends who were members of other districts were being approved to become ordained deacons provided they met all the requirement by the time our Annual Conference met in June. But the Spartanburg District superintendent, the highly respected civil rights leader and advocate for the homeless Dr. McKay Brabham, decided all of the other requirements had to be met before candidates could even appear before the District Committee on Ordained Ministry seeking the district's endorsement.

So, set back a year in my plans for my future, I went to Annual Conference and watched while my seminary buddies became ordained pastors.

The next year I repeated the process, anticipating June 1977 would be my time of ordination. By this time, the process for ordination was being rewritten. A new candidacy process was being enacted, and Dr. Brabham thought this would be required in my case.

Now, in fairness to Dr. Brabham, he had reasons to drag his feet where I was concerned. My theology was like a housefly—all over the place. You never know what a housefly might have landed on or stepped in before it lands on your plate ... or your church! I think he was giving me time to mature a bit (Penny is still waiting) and for my theology to settle down, and so once again I was delayed, or so I thought.

But then some colleagues on the Annual Conference's Board of Ordained Ministry told me Dr. Brabham was incorrect, that the new candidacy process would not get cranked up until the next year, and I should complete all the required paperwork assigned by their board. I was even declared psychologically fit, believe it or not.

And so in June 1977, I was finally ordained deacon. My job title at the church was changed from "Assistant to the Pastor" to "Associate Pastor." Friends at church quipped that the sign on my office door would not even have to be changed. I was still the "Ass. Pastor."

In July 1977, I was still feeling a bit paranoid. The other seminary students had been given documents from their home districts—a license to preach and a letter stating they had been approved for ministry—but I didn't have either of these. By this time, Dr. Brabham had become the pastor of a church in Columbia, and so I went by his new office to ask about those documents.

"Oh, yeah," he drawled. "Let me call the new Spartanburg District superintendent, Dr. Ted Walter." I sat there in his office as he and Ted talked.

"Ted, look at the minutes of our District Committee on Ordained Ministry's spring meeting and read me the names of the people we approved for ordination. ... Uh huh. ... OK. ... Uh huh. ... You don't see the name 'Arthur Holt' on that list? Well, could you scribble his name in the margin?"

Immediately after this phone call, Dr. Brabham filled out the required documents and I became an R.P. (Real Preacher).

I didn't tell anyone about this for a very long time. It wasn't that I was still paranoid, but all those people who were out to get me were!

But I did tell my new boss and mentor Dr. Jim Nates about what had happened. From then on, Jim has told others, "I guess you know that Arthur is just a marginal preacher."

The Residency Rebels

Early in my career as a pastor, it became church law that each pastor had to be involved in some type of continuing education—thirty contact hours per year. While most of us chafed at the bit a little when this was inaugurated, we all agreed it was badly needed.

I enrolled in a nine-month course on OD—organizational development—led by the Rev. Joe Alley and also in a unit of clinical pastoral education at a hospital early in my ministry, and both were so helpful to me.

Soon after continuing education for pastors was started, groups of clergy began meeting one day every month in support groups that were originally called "Residency II." Usually there was a group for every district in our annual conference. Some were aimed at specific interests like hiking, canoeing, or studying a theologian. Every month after the lunch break, each of us had the opportunity to share personal concerns or struggles in an atmosphere of trust and committed confidentiality. This was such an amazing thing to be a part of. I saw some times of great personal healing in people's lives.

In the last decade of my ministry, I was invited to join a group that went by the name of "Residency Rebels." We claimed not to care whether or not we reported our hours to the conference (but most of us did), and we invited a small group of people from all over the state to join us in Columbia. It was a diverse group, racially and gender inclusive, made up of young pastors starting out and pastors already retired and those in between. I think I got included because my former boss, Jim Nates, and a friend from college, Richard Allen, decided to invite me.

Never in my life was I so surrounded by such a talented bunch of advisors and encouragers. I have thought many times how I wished I had been with that same group of pastors for all the years of my ministry. The collective wisdom in that group was often life-saving and life-giving.

Often this was a safe place to vent frustrations over things going on in our parish.

Problems with children and teens could be safely shared. More than once we heard sad stories of painful divorce—spouses who couldn't take the fish bowl any longer, or people growing weary of moving every four to six years of their lives. Events in life had caused some of our participants to doubt themselves and God.

But in the Residency Rebels, they found understanding and wise counsel. This was also a place of great laughter as well.

So I say thanks to Richard, Doug, Jim, Cathy, Anthony, James the Less, Steve, Phil, David, Joel, Bill, Kristen, Mike, and others I am sure I left out.

Rev. Douglas Arthur Bowling

On April 5, 2016, seven months after he died very suddenly of a heart attack, some of Doug Bowling's preacher-friends met at a restaurant to tell our "Doug stories." We all had been so deeply touched by his life—and his death—that we felt compelled to hold our own post-funeral wake.

Our meeting was scheduled to be at Tommy's Ham House in Greenville at eight a.m., but a wreck at sunrise in downtown Greenville had taken out the electrical power at that restaurant, leaving us scrambling for our egg breakfasts. All of us traveling to the meeting—whether from Simpsonville, Spartanburg, or Clemson—encountered wrecks and traffic jams, and all this happened on a day when the skies were absolutely clear. Each of us thought maybe Doug was messing with us, once again having fun at our expense.

It is unquestionably true that no one has been more influential in the latter decades of my life than Doug Bowling. He had a sixth sense that enabled him to spot a person who was struggling with some personal or professional issue, and then he took that person on as a personal project, giving himself to that person in a therapeutic friendship. I was one of those projects. He became that big brother I must have always needed.

Doug arranged for me to join a coffee group, and he met with me one-on-one also. A few weeks after Doug died, I became so very thankful for the pain that had given me one of the best friends I had ever had. If I had the chance to live my life over and avoid the pain—but that avoidance would mean that I would not have had Doug as my friend—I'd choose to hurt all over again if it would give me my friend Doug. That's how important he was to me and how important he is to my life's story.

Doug's childhood was not a happy one. Without judging the family situation, let me say he found it necessary to leave home while he was still a teenager. He was taken in by the youth workers of his church. From then on, they were his parents, and their children were his siblings. Their home would be where he would spend his holidays, and when those parents died, Doug was listed as one of the survivors. As far as I know, Doug never had any further contact with his biological family—not his biological parents or siblings. That was one of Doug's strengths. Once he made a decision, he never looked back.

I was a sophomore at Wofford when I first met Doug. The Spartanburg district superintendent, in a flash of great wisdom, had assigned me to Fairmont UMC as student pastor. I am sure that the pastoral care from an immature nineteen-year-old was quite lacking! The next year the DS decided to put Fairmont on a charge with Ben Avon, meaning that Doug—twenty-five years old by then—would be their new pastor. Doug invited me to lunch to discuss Fairmont, and I told him exactly how he should conduct his ministry there. Doug was gracious, as I recall.

Ten years later we were re-introduced at a minister's We Care event at Union UMC in Irmo. I had completed seminary by then, and Doug told the entire group, "I am so glad I got to come here so I could meet Arthur Holt again!" That was the only hint I ever got that our previous meeting had been less than stellar in his opinion.

Back in the late 1990s, Doug and I were a part of a clergy support group that met in Columbia each month. This group was immensely important to me, and it gave our friendship the chance to grow. When I dropped out of the group because of the distance I was having to drive, Doug insisted I return to the group and always drove me to Columbia.

When we gathered on April 5 to tell our "Doug stories," the first thing we all remembered was Doug's rather "salty" vocabulary and his enjoyment in greeting each one of us by waving at us—with only one finger. His wife, Marlene, told about the time Doug was asked to come to Bishop Bethea's office and to bring his associate pastor Bill Kinnett with him. The bishop said he had received a complaint from a church member regarding Doug's cussing. Doug responded, "Damn! Did I do that?" The bishop advised Doug to be careful about his audience whenever he was tempted to cuss.

Some time after that meeting, Bishop Bethea walked up to Doug as they were both leaving a meeting, and putting his arm around Doug, asked him, "Doug, have you been cussing in front of the wrong people again?"

Doug replied, "Apparently."

If this notion offends anyone, then you don't know preachers! In Doug's case, it actually endeared people to him. People would say to him, "I've just got to come hear you preach!" When they did, they heard a powerful message.

I didn't know until shortly before his death that Doug was always very nervous before every sermon, so nervous that he was often sick on Saturdays and Sundays before he preached! It never showed.

One time God even used Doug's "vocabulary" to reach a very lonely, bitter, and grieving man. This story was told by Dr. John Simmons as part of his eulogy at Doug's funeral. The man's wife had a complicated illness, and her treatment was expensive and unsuccessful. Health-care personnel had been uncaring and insensitive. Bill collectors were harassing them. A neighbor across the street had baked some cupcakes as a gesture of love, but she was turned away. So she talked with her new pastor, Doug.

Doug took those cupcakes to the door, and without taking the time to find out who this visitor was who was knocking at his door, that man began to swear at God and to God and about God.

Dr. Simmons related, "Doug responded by telling the man to say that again. And again and again. Then they said it together, swearing and cursing over and over. After a while, they stopped, and Doug asked the man if he felt better. The frown on his face began to relax and the man said something to the effect that 'I didn't know anyone cared.' Doug said, 'I care and God cares.' The emotional healing began at that point, and a person who had been alienated from God and from the church and from life and from love began to experience reconciliation."

Doug wasn't a skilled laborer. Most often he called his friend George Riser whenever there was something needed, like a leaking faucet or trouble with his computer. Once Doug put a corner shelf up at the height of six feet, doing so by setting the shelf on top of a six-foot ladder. He and Marlene decided that it needed to be six inches lower, so Doug knew what to do. He took his ladder outside and cut six inches off each leg. Returning to the corner with his five-foot-six-inch ladder, he set the shelf on top of the ladder once again and installed it at the perfect height.

I had my stories to tell as well—like about the fact that Doug would call our house, and if Penny would answer the phone, he would always ask to speak with "sh**head" (I bet you can figure that out).

Then there was the time I was taking a car to the Ford dealership for repairs. As I was explaining the car problem to the service rep, my cell phone rang. Nobody called me on my cheap "burner" cell phone; I didn't use it that much back then. It was Doug calling. Doug never called me on my cell phone. I answered to hear his voice say, "Hey man. What's going on."

I told him where I was.

"Do you need a ride home?" he asked me and I said that I did not.

When he never got to the point, I finally asked him why he had called me and he said he hadn't! I had called him and then hung up without saying a word.

"Doug, I am sorry! I must have butt-dialed you by accident."

Doug replied, "Arthur, I am sick and tired of your ass calling me!"

Doug and his preacher buddies were always playing tricks on each other. But none were better than the ones played between Doug and the Rev. Gareth Scott. Many of us pastors had dealings with a wandering soul named Carl. Carl had a regular circuit. He would hitchhike from Columbia up to Tennessee and back, always knowing where United Methodist churches were. He was a huge but harmless man who was slightly tongue-tied. One evening he came upon Gareth inside the church in Union, South Carolina, and when Gareth yelled in reaction to the surprise of seeing Carl, Carl also yelled, saying "You scared me!" Carl would then say, "I wouldn't hurt no fwee."

On another occasion, Carl needed a ride to Columbia, and since Gareth was going there for a meeting, he offered to take Carl with him. He let Carl out of his car in the parking lot of Washington Street UMC, telling him to go to the office of the Rev. Doug Bowling, saying that his friend Gareth said to give him two nights' lodging and a new coat. Doug dutifully did. Later that year Gareth was reassigned to a church in Simpsonville. He gave his old church strict orders not to tell Carl where he had been moved.

Soon Carl returned to Doug's church, asking for assistance, but especially asking if he knew where Rev. Scott now lived. Not only did Doug tell him—he also bought Carl a bus ticket to Simpsonville.

That night Gareth found a familiar face pressed up against a window pane mouthing the words, "Found you!"

Perhaps something that tells a lot about Doug is how he and his lifelong friend the Rev. Ron Pettit met at Spartanburg Methodist College ("Junior College" as it was called back then). One Saturday, Doug was in the library studying when a huge athlete also came to the library. When the athlete couldn't find a book on the shelf he needed, he began to take out his frustrations on the librarian. The student ranted and raved and cursed at the woman until freshman Doug had quite enough.

"You will have to leave the library now!" Doug told the guy.

When the guy threatened to beat Doug up, Doug said, "You probably can whip me, but you are still going to leave the library now."

From behind a desk, a tough guy from Gaffney—Ron Pettit—stood up and said, "And after you have whipped him, you will have to whip me because you are leaving the library right now." Outnumbered, the big brute left the library, and Doug and Ron, who both later became United Methodist pastors, became lifelong buddies.

Grand Finale

Some years ago at a district meeting, some frustrated layperson asked the district superintendent, "When are you going to start sending us better pastors?"

The wise DS replied, "Just as soon as you start raising them."

We sometimes forget that part of the equation. Churches give birth to pastors and raise them, and the raising continues in every place we pastors move.

So often I read stories in church histories that tell about the pastors that have been appointed to their churches and how those pastors blessed the congregation. But I haven't read many books from pastors who want you to know the people and the churches that have shaped their lives, who have been there for us when the pastor or his/her spouse or children needed them. This is my way of acknowledging the gift God gave me when God allowed me to become a pastor. God called me to preach so my congregations could teach me about God's love.

For every person I wrote about, there are at least twice as many I could have included. Every place where I was appointed became an opportunity for me to grow—by getting to know God's good people who lived there. They taught me more about God!

Maybe another book will spring to life in me one day.

About the Author

The Rev. Arthur H. Holt is a retired United Methodist pastor who grew up in Spartanburg, South Carolina, and is a 1972 graduate of Wofford College. He earned his Master of Divinity from Lutheran Theological Southern Seminary in 1979 and has pastored churches across South Carolina. Married to his wife, Penny, for more than fifty years, they have two children and four grandchildren.

www.ingramcontent.com/pod-product-compliance
Lightning Source LLC
Chambersburg PA
CBHW032131090426
42743CB00007B/553